Sun Tzu The Art of Making Money:

Strategies for getting through a tough economy

Michael M. K. Cheung

Sun Tzu The Art of Making Money:

Strategies for getting through a tough economy

First Edition published by ALLYSKY LIMITED 2012

Copyright © Michael M. K. Cheung 2012

The author has asserted his moral right to be identified as the author of this work in accordance with the Copyrights, Designs and Patents Act 1988

All rights reserved under international and Pan-American Copyright Conventions. By payment of the required fees, you have been granted the non-exclusive rights to access and read the text of this book. No part of this text may be reproduced, transmitted, downloaded, decompiled, reverse engineered, or stored in any information storage and retrieval system, in any form or by any means whether electronic or mechanical, now known or hereinafter invented, without the express written permission of Michael M. K. Cheung and ALLYSKY Limited.

> ISBN-13: 978-1480089006
> ISBN-10: 1480089001

ACKNOWLEDGEMENTS

I'd like to take this opportunity to thank my family, friends and the people I have both worked with and who have all contributed greatly to the events in my life.

I would like to thank my copy editor Karen Carter, without her hard work and dedication to the project this book would not have been finished on time.

I would like to thank Sun Tzu for his wisdom and insight and Lionel Giles for his translation of The Art of War into English in 1910.

Finally I would like to thank my wife Ally for a lifetime of love and commitment.

Limit of Liability/Disclaimer of Warranty: While the Publisher and Author have used their best efforts in preparing this book, they make no representations or warranties with respects to the accuracy or completeness of the contents of this book and specifically disclaim any implied warranties of merchantability or fitness for a particular purpose. No Warranty may be created or extended by sales representatives or written sales materials. The advice and strategies contained herein may not be suitable for your situation. You should consult with a professional where appropriate. Neither the publisher nor the Author shall be liable for any loss of profit or any other commercial damages, including but not limited to special, incidental, consequential, or other damages.

Names, characters, businesses, places, events and incidents are either the products of the author's imagination or used in a fictitious manner. Any resemblance to actual persons, living or dead, or actual events is purely coincidental.

TABLE OF CONTENTS

Introduction ································1
I. Laying Plans ······························5
II. Waging War ····························37
III. Attack by Stratagem ····················51
IV. Tactical Dispositions ····················69
V. Energy ·································97
VI. Weak Points and Strong ················121
VII. Maneuvering ·························131
VIII. Variation in Tactics ···················137
IX. The Army on the March ················149
X. Terrain ································167
XI. The Nine Situations ····················175
XII. The Attack by Fire ····················190
XIII. The Use of Spies ·····················195
XIV. Conclusion ··························203

Introduction

In searching for the secret to how to improve my life by making more money, I came across the ancient wisdom of Sun Tzu. Sun Tzu was a general who lived in northeastern China around 2,500 years ago and was a master of military tactics. Such was his genius that his military tactics and thoughts eventually were put into writing so they could be passed down to other generations to come. Although the famous book, *The Art of War,* deals with situations on the battlefield and how one should apply them to a given situation, there is much wisdom in it that can be put to great use by those striving to be successful in modern life.

Even though much has changed since the time of Sun Tzu, we remain subjected to key forces that existed then. The human spirit and its strengths and weaknesses are still present, and the same forces of nature and economic cycles are still with us. While the names and faces have certainly changed, the game of success is still the same as it was 2,500 years ago.

Sun Tzu The Art of Making Money details how the ancient warrior's codified strategies can be leveraged so anyone can benefit from his wisdom.

Michael M. K. Cheung

Success is often measured by the amount of money one has, and money doesn't generally appear by chance. Most of us have only what we've managed to save. But the truth is even just $100 and the will and passion to choose your own destiny represent a pretty good place to start.

If you master just a fraction of Sun Tzu's wisdom you will be able to effect significant changes in your life.

I hope you enjoy reading and learning from the wisdom of Sun Tzu and wish you good luck in your future, wherever it may take you.

Michael M. K. Cheung

London

Sun Tzu The Art of Making Money

Michael M. K. Cheung

I. Laying Plans

Sun Tzu said: *The art of war is of vital importance to the State or nation.*

It is a matter of survival, that of life and death, a road either to safety or to ruin.

Therefore it is a subject of inquiry which can on no account be ignored.

The art of making money is of vital importance to the well-being of your bank account.

It is a matter of survival. Without cash in the bank you are exposed to the rough elements of the world in which you live. You must study the best ways for you to earn, save, and invest money if you wish to prosper.

Sun Tzu said: *The art of war has five factors that one must consider when looking at the situation that is placed in front of him in life:*

(1) The Moral Law

(2) Heaven

(3) Earth

(4) The Commander

(5) Method and Discipline

The MORAL LAW causes the people to be in agreement with their ruler so they follow him regardless of any danger they might face.

HEAVEN signifies times and seasons, day and night or hot and cold.

EARTH relates to the terrain and distances, danger and security, narrow passes or open ground, and the chances of life and death.

The COMMANDER stands for leadership that embodies attributes of wisdom, courage, kindness, and firmness.

METHOD AND DISCIPLINE relate to the chain of command and proper use of resources.

The Moral Law

You are at your best and most successful when you follow your passions and interests, your own Moral Law. Only then will your head and heart work as one. You are doing what you really want to do in life when you are focused solely on the task at hand. You wake up every morning feeling alive and buzzing with energy. When you are in agreement with your ruler (i.e., your head and your heart) you are ready to take on any challenge and can identify and succeed at the job that's best suited for you. Finding this perfect fit and earning income through it is the ideal way to fund your aspirations for wealth and success.

Heaven

Scholars of the art of making money carefully consider the workings of economic cycles. In the same way Heaven provides seasons, economic cycles provide changing economic times that fluctuate between boom and bust. Before you can take action regarding your finances, you must observe where you are in relation to the economic cycle. Are you in boom times or bust times? Once you know this you can develop an appropriate action plan.

Earth

When in bust times, the passages you navigate on Earth narrow and you must play it safe so you do not lose what you accumulated during boom times. Rather than take foolish risks with your capital during bust times, plan to buy quality defensive stocks such as pharmaceuticals, tobacco, food and beverages, and utilities rather than risky tech or other trendy stocks. Don't put all your money in one stock or sector as you build your platform of financial stability.

Also avoid working for the same company for a long time, expecting them to look after you into old age. Do something else on the side to build up your passive income streams and ensure that your skills don't become obsolete, and keep networking outside your company so you can explore better opportunities as they arise.

The Commander

You are the commander of your life, no one else. Don't blame others for failings you've experienced. If things are not going well, the only one responsible is you. As your own commander, you have the right to learn from such past mistakes and take steps to improve yourself and your life going forward.

Method and Discipline

Remember the Serenity Prayer; work every day to change the things you can change and accept those you cannot change.

When working toward positive change, watch what falls to the bottom line.

Take for example Joe, an average office worker. He brings home $1,000 a month, but spends $1,000 a month. What is his bottom line? Zero, zilch, nothing.

Don't be like Joe. Cut unnecessary expenses during bust times. Even during boom times, make a budget and stick to it. Abandon short-term self-gratification and avoid compulsive purchases such as an iPad and expensive running shoes or regular budget-breakers such as going out for dinner or drinks. Save extra cash instead to build a war chest for buying stocks and creating passive income streams.

When funds are available, Method and Discipline require the proper use of such funds. A key concept here is the triangle of wealth, also called the pyramid of wealth.

The Pyramid of Wealth

The base of the pyramid of wealth is the foundation of your wealth that keeps you afloat. The *Protection* element includes wills and various forms of insurance to cover health, property, life, disabilities, etc. This foundation should be put in place before you begin to accumulate wealth.

Wealth Accumulation is comprised of three parts:

Sun Tzu The Art of Making Money

(1) Savings and Accumulations

First, open an emergency fund such as a regular savings account and fund it over time with the amount it would take for you to live for six months. If Joe were smart he'd save up $6,000 (six times his monthly take-home) and keep it in his basic savings account.

Once your safety net is set up, then you can funnel some disposable income into the purchase of fixed income products such as CDs. Also consider investing in property or other options with typically solid returns such as an education fund, a retirement fund, or additional savings accounts. Putting money into your own education, for example, will ensure your ability to take advantage of new opportunities as they arise.

(2) Growth and Diversification

This segment consists of bonds, stocks, mutual funds, and exchange traded funds. Consider investing in these types of financial instruments with the help of a trusted broker.

(3) Speculation

This segment consists of potentially riskier investments

in options, futures, commodities, real estate, and the foreign exchange market.

At the top of the pyramid under *Wealth Distribution* is estate planning, through which you can take actions to distribute accumulated wealth as you see fit.

In the Beginning

It's clear from the pyramid of wealth that in order to take steps toward *Wealth Accumulation* and ultimately *Wealth Distribution* you must first establish your *Protection* and then funnel additional income into appropriate wealth-building channels. In order to accomplish any of this, of course, you need to find a way to trade your time and energy for money. Refer to the earlier section on following your passions under The Moral Law heading for insights into how you can find the job that would be most satisfying for you.

With your earned income in hand, apply the Method and Discipline needed to follow the Chain of Command presented by the pyramid of wealth. Plan to build the base first and then the middle sections and then finally put the capstone on last. The rate at which you do this matters little. Your efforts toward following these steps make all the difference.

Sun Tzu The Art of Making Money

Sun Tzu said: *Every general should know these five components: he who knows them well can be victorious; he who is ignorant of them will fail.*

Below is a brief review of the five components you should know well in order to be successful:

The Moral Law

Take time to identify your passions. Know your strengths and play to them. Know your weaknesses and guard them while you work to improve them.

Think with your head and your heart as ultimate power is achieved when bother are in alignment with your goals. When you are fully committed and your head and heart are in alignment, then you can become unstoppable.

Heaven

Learn to identify where you are in the economic cycle.

In boom times, you can afford to take more risks, plan for expansion, or invest in tech or growth stocks or in start-ups or initial public offerings (IPOs).

In bust times, cut back on fixed-cost items and consider investing instead in safe stocks tied to everyday items such as pharmaceuticals, food and beverages, etc.

Earth

Acquire the skills you need to navigate difficult times. Consider taking a course in accounting and bookkeeping or in sales. The world has become one big marketplace; perhaps learning a new language would pay off in your chosen career.

Stop and listen to other people and pay attention to changes in the world around you. Consider which of your current skills need to be updated and if you need to acquire new skills.

The Commander

A good commander manages things well. Learn the pyramid of wealth to have a clear plan of attack to follow. Next, acquire money management skills so you can effectively fund your efforts. Spend less than you earn. Pay yourself first by putting the first 10 percent of your income into a savings account. Pay for things with cash rather than credit cards. If you use a credit card, pay off its balance every month.

Also learn about risk management so you can effectively assess the risk of any situation.

As an investor, don't invest money you can't afford to lose. Don't remortgage the house to invest in a friend's business or take out your life savings and put it into one stock. A good rule of thumb is to invest no more than five percent of your money in any one stock or investment venture.

Chain of Command

Follow the chain of command presented by the pyramid, starting at the base. This foundation, the least risky and safest part of the pyramid, will ensure that you put adequate protections in place for yourself and your family.

With that foundation in place you can start the process

of building your wealth. Don't be tempted to take shortcuts you believe will lead to instant wealth. Trading futures or even buying stocks on margin, for example, can be very effective but require a certain level of skill and a good understanding of risk management. Acquire the necessary background, knowledge, and skills first.

Sun Tzu said: *Therefore, in your discussions, when seeking to determine the military conditions, let us compare and contrast the issues.*

Which of the two rulers has the Moral law?

The two rulers are the head and heart. Do you follow your head or your heart, or both? If your head and heart are in agreement, chances are good you're heading in the right direction.

How many times have you been held back when your mind was focused on attaining a certain goal but your heart was not?

Mike, an average lawyer, doesn't like his job but likes the money and prestige that go with it. He also likes that he's pleasing his father by pursuing a career in law.

When Mike was growing up he really wanted to be a painter, but his father didn't agree with that path because he thought painters were not held in high regard by the general public. He encouraged Mike to become a lawyer instead. So Mike went to law school instead of art school.

While Mike's head was following what he thought was right, in his heart he was disappointed. He became an average lawyer and now hates every minute of it.

How many times have you been held back when your heart was focused on attaining a certain goal but your mind was not?

Sue, a passionate entrepreneur, sells baskets she makes out of bamboo. Although it takes her three weeks to make each basket, she sells them for only $15 each. Though her heart was in the right place when she decided to do what she loves and build a business around it, she failed to think through her business plan and charge enough so she can make a living through her sales.

Michael M. K. Cheung

Of the two rulers, which has the most capability?

Which is your strongest asset, your head or your heart?

Some people are very analytical and logical. Other people work from the heart.

If you are analytical and logical, you may want to focus on the finance part of your business and hire a passionate people person to focus on creative aspects of it such as marketing. If you work from the heart, you may be happiest in marketing or even sales.

Given Heaven and Earth, where are the advantages to be found?

Given the current economic environment in which you live, would it make more sense for you to work for someone or to be self-employed? To buy defensive stocks, or to focus on commodities?

Sarah, a fluent speaker of various Chinese dialects and very much a people person, went to China and set up a company to help U.S. businesses negotiate deals with

Chinese suppliers of raw materials. She acted as an intermediate agent, following her heart as she helped U.S. businesses connect with businesses in China.

Bill, a finance guy, opted to buy into the raw materials market in China instead. Both business people had foreseen the same economic boom that would take place in China but acted differently based on their own strengths.

Of the two sides, on which has the most rigorous discipline been applied?

Whether you are a logical thinker or of the heart, when pursuing any business, venture, or task you must be disciplined in your approach. Focus your efforts to the best of your abilities. Commit to achieving a high level of success. Stay disciplined and keep moving forward.

Which of the armed forces are stronger?

Always know your strongest skills and work with them. Don't be afraid to delegate tasks to others when they require skills that are not among your strongest.

On what side are captains and foot soldiers more highly trained?

Again, keep in mind your strengths and weaknesses and operate based on your strengths.

In which military is there the greater reliability for both reward and punishment?

In which areas have you excelled and in which areas have you failed?

Change habits that in the past have led to less-than-optimal results. Avoid doing the same actions over and over simply because you are set in your routine. You will never see improved results until you identify and pursue what's most effective.

Do something in a different way to see new change. Consider something from a new angle or learn a new set of skills. Even driving a different route to work can help you see things in a new way.

Once you've identified what works well, stick with it and focus on improving its implementation and results.

Sun Tzu said: *Given these seven concerns one can forecast victory or defeat.*

The more analysis you do, the better your chances of success. Keep in mind you can refine your business model and plan before you have to commit any resources to them. Modern tools used in the business world for forecasting likely victory or defeat include SWOT (strengths, weaknesses, opportunities, and threats) analysis, pros and cons lists, business plans, and cost-benefit analysis.

SWOT analysis identifies the objective of a business venture or project as well as the internal and external factors that help or hinder the achievement of that objective.

The following line items are considered via SWOT analysis:

Strengths: characteristics that put a business or project at an advantage

Weaknesses: characteristics that put a business or project at a disadvantage

Opportunities: opportunities available to a business or project

Threats: external factors that threaten the success of a business or project

Pros and Cons Lists can provide a good view of ideal and less-than-ideal courses of action. Consider, for example, possible pros and cons of getting a tattoo:

Pros

- It will look cool
- It will make me stand out more
- It will help me fit in at college
- It will help me express something I like
- It will help me express my sense of style
- It might turn into a hobby

Cons

- It will be painful to acquire
- It will be difficult to remove
- It may not look all that great
- It will be expensive to acquire
- It may lead to an infection
- It may hinder my ability to get a job

Now consider possible pros and cons of starting a business:

Pros

- You will be the boss
- You will have the flexibility to determine your own hours
- You will not have to deal with office politics, at least not among higher-ups
- You will gain experience in a variety of business areas such as IT, sales, marketing, finance, etc.
- You will determine your work pace
- You will determine your work environment

- You will do work that you want to do

- You will have the potential to earn more money than you might be earning now

- You will have the opportunity to build something you can pass onto your children

- You will make a contribution to your local community

Cons

- You will need to work hard seven days a week with little or no breaks for holidays

- Your income will be unknown, unpredictable, and unreliable, at least at first, with no steady pay checks

- You will risk losing your savings and increasing your personal debt

- Your success will not be guaranteed

- You will not receive as much acknowledgement of your efforts or encouragement or guidance

Business Plans are designed to focus efforts on exactly how specific ventures will be run. Details such as the product or service a business will sell as well as how sales and marketing, accounting, staffing, payroll, and revenue generation and collection will be managed are documented in a business plan, giving you a clear roadmap as well as a valuable tool for communicating with possible lenders or investors.

Cost-benefit analysis provides a systematic process for calculating and comparing likely benefits and costs of a project.

Consider Dan, who runs his own taxi company. Dan has 100 cars in his fleet and wants to upgrade the tires on each car to a better brand. Each new tire will cost $200.

Cost: ($200 x 4 tires) x 100 = $80K

Benefits: In addition to the benefits of new and better tires such as improved and safer vehicle performance, the new tires on Dan's fleet will lead to better gas mileage that equates to an anticipated savings on gasoline over one year of $100K.

These analysis results reassure Dan that his plan to

upgrade the tires makes good business sense and represents a wise investment.

Sun Tzu said: *The general that listens to my advice and acts upon it will conquer. The general that does not listen to my advice or act upon it will suffer a great defeat.*

Taking steps to conduct analysis but then disregarding its results will result in failure.

Ed, for example, wanted to start a business. Upon completion of his business plan he found he needed $150K to start. Foolishly, Ed ignored that fact and started with $50K of his own money and another $50K from his bank. Nine months down the line he ran out of money. Not only did his bank refuse to lend him any more money, it demanded immediate payment on his loan.

Had Ed raised the $150K his business needed prior to embarking on this project, he may have been successful. Unfortunately, Ed didn't listen to and act upon the findings of his own analysis.

Mary did some research and found that XCom Corp

stock was worth $5 a share but was trading at $8. Her friend, Jane, told her it was going to $17. Jane remortgaged her house and bought in at $8. Mary thought $8 was too expensive but rather than listen to her research she got carried away by her friend's excitement and bought at $12.

The next day XCom Corp stock sold off heavy and its price dropped to $7. Mary considered selling before the price dropped to $5, but Jane convinced her to wait as she was sure it was still going to $17. Mary disregarded her research again and waited for the price to go back up, but it never did. Instead it went to $5 and, when the CEO disclosed the company had lost a big order and was going bankrupt, the stock went to $0.

Listen to your research and act accordingly.

Sun Tzu said: *While listening to my advice, be ready to follow any helpful circumstances over and beyond that of the ordinary rules.*

Sometimes special situations occur in which you may need to go beyond the ordinary rules. If a particularly strong stock has fallen too far due to general market conditions you may be able to purchase blue chip stocks at a bargain price. You may then consider purchasing such stocks with more than the generally recommended five percent of your total asset value.

If in business a competitor has gone bankrupt you might take over his stores to add to your own or buy up the best stores only. Any of these unusual strategies make sense in special situations.

Sun Tzu Said: *When circumstances are favorable, one should adapt one's plans to keep up with the new improved situation.*

Again, when the economic cycle changes modify your plans to take advantage of such new circumstances. Sometimes you have to go from defensive to offensive, for example, when going from bust to boom times. If you own a business, this might involve taking on new staff or opening new stores. If you're an investor, this might mean selling defensive stock and buying growth stocks. On the personal front, you might want to go back to school, take steps to get a new qualification, or begin a new career.

Sun Tzu The Art of Making Money

Sun Tzu Said: *All conflicts are based on deception.*

Deception is usually seen as something that is bad, but in the art of making money it can be a vital tool. Deception in the art of making money often involves possessing an asset your competition lacks and using it in surprising ways.

Since success is often also directly correlated to information flow and the protection of it, consider these examples:

A business that makes microchips keeps a new design hidden until right before its new product's launch so competitors can't copy the design until after the market has already been cornered.

An inventor keeps his invention quiet until he's registered his design with the patent office.

A trader on the financial markets keeps his position hidden so other traders can't sell against him and cost him money.

An investor remains quiet about a new opportunity until he's bought as much as he can before the price increase he confidently anticipates.

Non-disclosure agreements are commonly used in business to protect intellectual assets.

All these examples reflect the importance of keeping important information hidden away.

Sun Tzu Said: *Hence, when able to attack, we must seem inept; when using our forces, we must seem lethargic; when we are near, we must make the enemy believe that we are far away; when we are far away, we must make him think we are near.*

Posturing is a vital element to success. People read body language whether they are conscious of this practice or not. Strong body language can send out a message of confidence and dependability, even when one is feeling down.

On the other hand, using body language to project a possible weakness or need for guidance can lead to the assumption that one is less powerful. However, such an assumption can also lead an adversary to reveal his true position or to offer aid he hadn't been planning to provide.

People who remain unaware of their body language and what it reveals about themselves are considered by others to be so easy to read they can be quickly played and possibly duped. Work on your body language so you can convince others to think whatever you want them to believe. Such efforts will help lead you to more victories in challenging situations and ensure you won't be easily deceived.

Sun Tzu Said: *Entice the enemy closer with bait. Simulate disorder, and then crush him.*

Bait-and-switch tactics fall under this section but are fraudulent. Focus instead on your ability to confuse your competitors by making them believe you are less than competent and then surprising them with your preparation, confidence, and abilities.

Sun Tzu Said: *When the enemy is secure at all points, be prepared for him. If he is of superior strength, evade him.*

Michael M. K. Cheung

When the competition has superior strength you are wise to find new ways to succeed.

Lisa's competitor at the restaurant next door cooks and sells exceptionally good burgers, so she opened an exceptional vegetarian restaurant instead.

Steve is a lawyer who carved out a niche for himself as a specialist in trademarks and patents.

Kristi, a successful investor, focuses her time, energy, and investments on less popular commodities such as grains like rice and corn while most of her peers continue to invest in more traditional commodities such as precious metals and crude oil.

Rich, a trader, has learned it can pay handsomely to sit on one's hands and not buy when everyone else is selling.

Sun Tzu The Art of Making Money

Sun Tzu Said: *If your opponent is of excitable nature, then you must seek to irritate him. Create the illusion of weakness, which will lead him to become arrogant.*

If your business competitor is overly confident, gain a tactical advantage by keeping a low profile.

Consider Theo, a wealthy U.K. investor who bought a popular purveyor of ladies' lingerie. The owner of a much larger company selling similar products, overly confident due to his business's long-time top spot in the market, took no notice while Theo quietly built his company until it not only competed directly with the established retailer but surpassed it in sales for many years.

Sun Tzu Said: *If your enemy is trying to rest then keep him unsettled.*

To remain successful, your competitor needs to rest at times. Be aware of this and time your strongest moves when the competition has its guard down. Wait until after a big announcement from your competitor to counter with one of your own.

Sun Tzu Said: *If your enemy forces are cohesive, break them apart.*

In the same way it's easier to tackle a large task by breaking it down into smaller parts, it's easier to get ahead in an organization or cope with a competitor when you deal with one person or one aspect of your area of expertise at a time. When investing, focus on a particular type of investment, educate yourself about every aspect of it, and keep your investments targeted within that realm.

Sun Tzu Said: *When your enemy does not expect you, you must launch your attack and thus catch him of guard.*

Target the market niche your competitor is neglecting. Focus on personal skills development while your friends are focused on partying. Invest in commodities when most other investors are buying tech stocks.

Sun Tzu Said: *Military strategies which give you the edge and thus lead you to victory must remain secret in order for them to be effective.*

Sun Tzu The Art of Making Money

Just as wise inventors keep their inventions secret until they're patented, fully developed, and ready to take the market by storm, keep your ideas and plans private until you're fully prepared to disclose and act upon them.

Sun Tzu said: *Before a battle is fought, the wise general must consider all the issues that are presented in the battlefield.*

The unwise general who loses his battle has considered only a few of the important issues before he launches his attack.

He who analyzes more issues will be gifted with victory.

He who considers but a few will have defeat handed to him.

One can foresee who is likely to win or lose given how they prepare for battle. A general who does no analysis of the issues will be defeated as likely as night follows day.

Michael M. K. Cheung

II. Waging War

Sun Tzu said: *In the theatre of war, there are thousands of cavalry and mail-clad soldiers which have enough provisions to carry them many miles. The cost on the front line and at home will reach the total of thousands of ounces of silver per day. Such is the cost of running an army of 100,000 soldiers.*

Be sure up front that you've accumulated enough resources to complete a task before you undertake it.

If you want to become a doctor, for example, calculate how much money you'll need and how many years it will take to reach this goal. Then assess whether you have the stamina, strength, and financial resources to reach this goal.

If you'd like to start a business of any kind you need to be certain you have the funds to invest up front, the network to ensure future investments as needed, the skills and knowledge required, plus the energy that will be required to make your business a success.

Investing also requires an assessment of available resources until new investments start to provide adequate returns.

Sun Tzu said: *When you engage in actual fighting, if victory is long in coming, you will exhaust all your resources and the resources of the Nation will not be equal to the strain brought onto it.*

Starting any venture or taking on any task can result in a protracted experience. Prepare for the fact your various types of resources may be strained and surround yourself with those who are willing and able to help.

If you are starting a business that will take at least three to five years to become profitable, make sure you have enough money to live off during that time.

If you want to sue someone for property damage, make sure you can afford to take him to court. Even if your claim against him is right, you might win only enough to cover the damages and not your legal fees, and the case may drag on for longer than expected. In such a case, you might lose too much money to make the case worth pursuing.

Sun Tzu Said: *When you have battled long and hard and your supplies are exhausted and your weapons are of no use, you will find other factions will rise up and take up arms against you. Then no matter how wise or able, you will not be able to prevent your own demise.*

When you're in a protracted situation in which your resources have become exhausted your enemies will try to strike you down.

Consider Glen, who remortgaged his house so he could go back to college to study to be a lawyer. Overall, he borrowed $50K for the three-year program. But before he could get a job he became ill from a condition that required months of recovery and eventually the bank foreclosed on his house.

Ann wanted to expand her small business and borrowed against her house to do so, but the expansion didn't work out. The new product she developed didn't sell well and the bank recalled the loan, forcing her into bankruptcy.

Tim bought some stock of Company Xyz. He knew it was worth the $50 a share he paid for it but after he bought in its price kept dropping $1 a day. He had no more money to invest and had to close out his position. Of course after that a take-over bid was announced and the stock jumped to $55 a share.

Sun Tzu said: *In war only fools rush in but equally delays have never been associated with being clever either.*

Consider this old saying: "There is a dumb dollar, there is a smart dollar, and then there is just a dollar."

Chip makes $100 a day by taking away other peoples' unwanted items and selling them for scrap.

Meanwhile Chad makes $100 a day writing very sophisticated software code that controls a new-age robotic system.

💰 + 🤵 = The Smart Dollar

At the end of the day both these jobs produce $100 in income. Whether this objective is achieved via a "dumb" (i.e., simple) way or a "smart" (i.e., challenging) way really doesn't matter as long as the goal is reached.

It takes less time and effort to improve an existing type of product than to create an entirely new type of product. There's nothing wrong with opening another coffee shop. You simply need to have a unique selling point that improves the typical products or services most people associate with coffee shops.

Sun Tzu said: *No country has benefited from having a protracted campaign in the arena of warfare.*

Do not spend all your time at war with those around you. You can be right but you don't have to impose your ideas on others all the time. Don't waste your energy and resources trying to convince others that your way is the correct way.

Don't spend all your resources fighting battles with your business competitors. Most of your resources should be put into developing and improving your product or service.

Don't try to beat the stock market at every turn. The market will always win; it's bigger than any one trader. Focus on winning small battles on a regular basis but accept when you make a poor call and be willing to adjust your strategies to take on a new challenge.

Sun Tzu said: *When one has made themselves conversant with the evils of war only then can one know all the most profitable ways to gain from it.*

Sometimes the only way that a business can grow is at the expense of a smaller competitor. A mid-sized business may need to buy out a smaller competitor quickly before another competitor does and creates a much larger company. The owner of the mid-sized company needs to be aware of this reality and be willing to act upon it to succeed.

In the process of such an acquisition, long-time employees at either organization may need to be let go. Again, the owner must be willing to make such cuts, regardless how difficult, in order to keep his business profitable.

Sun Tzu said: *The skilled general does not need to construct an extra set of defenses or double his supplies.*

Consider what I call the "max-min principle": It is just as important to maximize the benefit as it is to minimize costs associated with that benefit. This is also known as the "min-max principle." Reduce costs expended—whether in the form of time, money, physical effort, or mental effort—while working to maximize the results and benefits of the task at hand.

Michael M. K. Cheung

John, a smart student, realizes he can't possibly ace every exam he has to take during finals week, so he focuses his studying on his weakest subjects to ensure he at least passes those exams and can go on to the next level in that coursework. Meanwhile he easily passes and advances in his strongest classes.

Kim, a real estate agent, is considering leasing rather than buying a new car. Leasing would minimize the need for a significant initial capital outlay and would allow her to get the larger, nicer car she needs for driving clients around town to look at properties.

Sun Tzu said: *When you go to war you should bring resources with you but always look to forage on the enemy.*

If you are a business owner consider buying inventory from bankrupt businesses or targeting their customers.

When buying any type of real estate, check with local banks to find discounted properties, especially those whose owners have gone bankrupt or must sell for other reasons.

Sun Tzu said: *If your state treasury is suffering from poverty then your army will be underfunded and your people impoverished.*

Be careful not to over-extend your reach with regard to your resource base.

Ben had a mortgage of $250K but his wife wanted a much bigger house. Last year was really good and as the top sales guy in his firm Ben got a big enough bonus to put down a $50K deposit for a new home. This year, however, the market took a turn for the worse, Ben has sold much less, and now he's struggling to pay the mortgage and his house is under water, with negative equity.

Tom's business was doing well so he took out a lease on a new office to accommodate anticipated growth. While his rent bill doubled the market went south and he wasn't able to hire as many new team members as anticipated or generate enough sales to pay the new monthly lease.

Alice, a property developer, had four houses in Florida on the portfolio that were doing well. She stepped things up a level and her bank helped her buy another six houses. These properties were in Arizona, however, and the extra distance and associated travel expenses made it too difficult for Alice to keep up with all her properties.

Sun Tzu said: *An army that is far away will require much resources from its homeland.*

Living close to the city in which you work can be expensive, but commuting a long way can take its toll. A careful choice of location is required so you have enough time, money, and energy to enjoy yourself after your bills have been paid and your savings funded.

Location and other costs also must be considered when setting up an office or buying real estate. Be sure to assess all related issues such as taxes, possible economic downturns, and your backup plan in case things don't work out.

Michael M. K. Cheung

Sun Tzu said: *When the homeland has it resources drained to support a faraway army then famine will ensue and so will a drop in maintenance of public services.*

When you've run into more obstacles than anticipated and your morale is running low you may begin to feel apathetic. Depression may even set in. Guard against this happening and do what you can to prevent it via healthy habits related to your diet, sleep, and exercise. Also be sure to ask for help when you need it.

If your business has waged a long campaign that has not been especially successful staff morale may become low and the business may suffer. Find ways to turn this around as quickly as possible.

When you're exhausted and drained mentally and physically, you are more likely to make bad judgment calls. Such mistakes can be very expensive. When the market is giving you a beating don't keep on going at it, take a break to reassess your strategy, returning only after you've had time to recuperate and prepare a new plan of attack.

Sun Tzu said: *When the resources have been stripped from the homeland the people will suffer even more and will have a third of their money taken by the government so they can pay for someone to fix the broken chariots and buy new horses and swords and bows. Adding in for replacement of supplies you can consider that 40 percent of the homeland income will be diverted to the government treasury for the paying of all these costs.*

If you work to a point at which you're trying to do too many things and getting run down you'll end up spending money to get medical help, buy medicine, even go to therapy sessions. Prevent this by pacing yourself and taking care of your health from the start. Investments in your health always pay off.

The cost of replacing staff in your business can also be very expensive. Take steps to keep morale high in your office so your business doesn't have to experience such costly disruptions.

Building your investment capital takes time but can be lost in a blink of an eye due a few bad decisions. Guard against this happening by taking time to rest and reassess your investment strategy.

Sun Tzu said: *A wise general who understands these matters will forage on the enemy instead of taking from his homeland. He will consider that one cart of the enemy's provisions is worth as much as 10 times his own. He need not drain his own supplies and put strain on his countrymen when he can devastate his enemy by taking from them.*

Look for and take advantage of opportunities to keep and invest as much of your earned income as possible. Seek out employers who offer free employee training or subsidize employees' educations. Find a less expensive place to live, learn to cook rather than eat out all the time, and take investing classes so you can invest wisely.

Sun Tzu said: *In warfare you must be able to cajole your men into battle by letting them know of the rewards they will gain when the enemy is defeated. Promise spoils of war to your men who fight with heart. Then capture and use whatever resources you find on the battlefield, be it equipment or men,* *to substantially improve your own resources as well as your soldiers' morale, loyalty, and resolve.*

Take care of those who help you succeed. Make sure they know they are appreciated and share with them the many tangible rewards of your success.

Sun Tzu said: *In battle one should strive for a short campaign and a great victory.*

In any project or campaign the objective is to reach your goal by utilizing the least amount of resources.

SMART is a mnemonic to help set such important objectives:
Specific – make it well defined
Measurable – know when it is achieved (i.e., define the finish line)
Achievable – identify other examples
Realistic – consider your resources such money, time, and knowledge
Time-bound – set a timeframe for the project (e.g., one year)

The SMART criteria can be used as a framework before the start of any new project. When learning to drive, for example, one of your objectives may be to get a driver's license as quickly as possible.

Specific goal = Get driver's license

Measurable result = Examiner gives me a license

Achievability proof = My friends and family members have drivers' licenses

Realistic plan, including resources = I can invest two days per week in learning to drive, read books from the library or documents online about driving, and use some of the $2K my parents are paying toward my driving lesions. Since $20 a lesson x 40 hrs = $800 I have enough money to try again if I fail the first time.

Timeframe = I think it will take me 40 hours to prepare for and pass the driving test. If I spend two hours a week then I'll spend 20 weeks or five months learning to drive.

Consider another scenario:

Specific goal = You want to open a coffee shop

Measurable result = Your coffee shop is open and profiting from customers' business

Achievability proof = You and many others bought coffee from a coffee shop every day when you were at college but in your hometown there is no coffee shop but there are plenty of people who will pay to drink good coffee.

Realistic plan, including resources = You have $100K from an investor and you have three years' experience working in a successful coffee shop.

Timeframe = It will take six months to find and lease a suitable storefront as well as refit and stock the shop.

When considering possible business investments, determine not only how much of a return you'll earn on your money but when you will receive such returns.

Max offers you a business investment he promises will return millions in profit or more. His plan: to invent a teleporter.

Gil has a business that recycles trash from peoples' homes. He needs money to double his capacity via the purchase of additional vehicles. He promises an 18 percent return on your money within two years.

SMART for Max's teleporter invention:

S = Max wants to build a teleporter.

M = When his machine is able to teleport a human being 100 yards, Max will have successfully invented a teleporter.

A = No one has come close to building a teleporter before.

R = Max needs millions of dollars, decades of time, as well as a brilliant mind and years of experience in the field, none of which Max has.

T = Max has no idea when, if ever, he might succeed.

Sun Tzu The Art of Making Money

<u>SMART for Gil's Recycling Waste Company</u>

S = Gil wants to buy additional vehicles and hire more drivers to expand his trash-collection business and increase his profits.

M = When Gil has doubled his fleet from 25 to 50 vehicles and run the larger fleet for at least a year with increased profits he will have been successful in this project.

A = Gil has already earned revenue in his established business.

R = Gil has a business plan and already has customers and buyers. He just needs more vehicles and drivers.

T = Once Gil gets the funds he knows he can have 25 new vehicles within one month and can hire more drivers, which may take up to two months. He has projected through analysis that his business growth will lead to enough profits that will enable him to repay your investment with an 18 percent return within two years.

Sun Tzu said: *A general is the leader of men; their fate is in his hands. In the best interest of the whole army, the general must be as objective as possible when dealing with a single soldier.*

Remember you are responsible for the outcome of every project you undertake.

Michael M. K. Cheung

You are responsible for your personal and financial happiness. The actions that you take will define your successes in various areas of your life.

As a business owner, CEO, or managing director, you are responsibility for whether your company is successful. Your employees depend on you for many things.

As an investor you decide whether to buy or sell a stock or do nothing. Don't let the market or public opinion dictate what you do. And don't blame your broker when things don't always work out.

Think wisely, plan accordingly, and lead yourself into victory on every front.

III. Attack by Stratagem

Sun Tzu said: *In the art of war, it is better to capture the enemy whole and intact; if you destroy it then you have won but lost the prize. The General who has mastered the art of war will destroy as little as possible in order to win, keeping as many things of value intact as possible.*

Debbie wants to be the best salesperson in her company so she takes subtle steps to sabotage the efforts of the other sales teams. As a result the company does poorly, impacting not only her own sales team but her own ability to succeed.

At another company, Cindy designs a fun competition through which the winning sales team gets a tacky trophy to display each month. In this way she generates a positive work environment and a healthy competitive spirit that leads to improved overall business results for everyone.

Sun Tzu said: *Do not consider yourself a great general of high of excellence if you have to fight in order to conquer. You are elite if you win instead by breaking the enemy's spirit and resistance without laying down a single fighting blow. The ideal is to prevent the enemy from executing its plan. Second* *best is to stop enemy forces from being deployed. Only if this fails must you engage the enemy on the battlefield. The worst policy is to lay siege to enemy city walls. Laying siege to the enemy's city walls will be a costly exercise that will take many months and will consume much of your resources.*

Fighting should be a last resort when striving to achieve a desired result. When faced with a challenging situation, project, or task the best course is to win without having to use or commit any resources to a struggle.

When at all possible, take the path of least resistance and effort. Keep your resources intact and take the toughest path only as a last resort when all other options have been explored.

Keri analyzes 500 stocks and buys 50, each of which pays dividend yields of four percent. She reads reports for all of these stocks on a regular basis and jumps in to buy and sell them several times a day.

Ken analyzes 500 stocks but picks only the top 10. After watching and waiting for them to get lower than normal he buys them when it makes sense and holds them for one year. He then reassesses his position once a year and adjusts his strategy as needed. Overall Ken earns a similar return as Keri but he invests much less time and effort as he successfully maintains his portfolio.

If you can't get a raise at work don't start looking to retrain in a new field, focus on improving the skills you already have. If such efforts don't result in a better situation in your present job, use your local networking efforts and improved skills sets to find a better job.

Sun Tzu said: *A general who is not able to control his emotions will be easily angered into launching an attack, the result of which is that 30 percent of his men will be killed and the city will remain untaken.*

If you can't control your emotions then they will control you. When you think emotionally you will become less objective. Remember your actions have consequences.

Martin purchases a stock based on a tip from a friend. Martin makes a large purchase of about $10K on XYZ stock and pays $10 a share for it. The next week the stock has fallen to $8 and he's pretty annoyed with the fact that the tip hasn't worked out. Determined to "get even" with the market he buys another $20K at $8. The next day the stock has fallen again to $6. Martin blows his top and takes the rest of his life savings of $40K and buys the next day at $5.50. At the end of the week the CEO announces that the company is going bankrupt. Martin loses all his money and his wife threatens to leave him if he ever buys another stock again.

Had Martin cut his losses when he was down to $8 and gotten out rather than trying to get even, he would have taken a $2K loss rather than a $70K loss.

Instead he let his emotions get in the way, which caused him to become reckless and lose all his savings.

Sun Tzu said: *A skilled general will render the enemy's troops inert without any fighting, take their cities without laying siege to them, and plan for and conduct a victorious, short campaign.*

Apply strategy before taking action. Before jumping into a new career, network with people in that field and talk to them about their experiences. Ask for advice on the best route for you to take based on your experience, interests, and skills. Investigate the pros and cons of your plan and use the analysis tools described earlier in this book to make sure you're making the best decision possible. Then plan your strategy and take action.

Sun Tzu said: *A general who can win without losing a single man and thus keep his forces intact is of elite standard. He has mastered the method of engaging the enemy with the use of strategy.*

Consider these everyday examples:

Jim spent eight weeks planning his family's vacation to the Grand Canyon and then two weeks enjoying the trip with his family.

Gary spent eight months planning his new business sales campaign and then two weeks executing it with great success.

Missy spent eight months planning her investments, researching them thoroughly. She then spent two weeks making her investments and earned a very tidy profit.

All these cases involved the use of wise assessments and planning prior to action, a sure way to succeed in any venture.

Sun Tzu said: *In war one should consider one's numerical position. If one has 10 times as many resources as the enemy then he can surround him. If five times as many resources he can fight him, but if one has only twice as many resources then he should divide his resources into two parts.*

Available resources often dictate which actions can be taken.

Winnie has $100K and hires an A-list celebrity to endorse her product. Her competitor, Belle, has only $10K and is able to hire only a C-List celebrity. It's easy to predict which competitor will launch well against her competition.

Lilly has $50K and hires a B-list celebrity to endorse her product. Anita, her competitor, has $10K to hire a C-list celebrity. Either of these competitors may put up a good fight against the other.

Byron has $20K but opts to hire a C-list celebrity for only $10K to endorse his product because he knows his main competitor can only spend $10K to do the same. Rather than spend all of his funds, he sets some aside in case his initial campaign is less successful as his competitor's and he needs to supplement it with other promotional efforts.

Sun Tzu said: *If one's forces are equally matched then he can engage the enemy. However if he has fewer forces he should avoid his enemy. If he is much smaller then he should retreat from him.*

Depending on the size of your resources and the task at hand you have three choices:

1) Attack
2) Avoid and Hide
3) Retreat

If you are equally as talented as your colleague then go head to head for that promotion.

If you are not quite as good then you might be better off staying in your position.

If you are really poor at what you do, then you should

retreat and focus on sharpening your skills.

If you have the same money and resources as your main competition then feel free to go on the offensive.

If you have slightly less money and resources then build your business in an area in which your competitor does not strong have a strong presence.

If you are much weaker then build your business far from his where your services or products are not yet available.

Sun Tzu said: *Despite occasional exceptions to the rule, a smaller force will very likely lose to a larger force.*

Both you and your competitor enter into a foreign market to expand your chains of women's shoe stores. Unfortunately you are going to lose if they have 50 shops for every one of yours.

You invest in a company that sells eco-friendly corn, but

your competitor spends ten times more money producing and promoting its genetically modified corn. Your competitor will have the upper hand.

In both cases, cut your losses and move on to your next plan.

Sun Tzu said: *A country that has a strong general will be safe from his enemy but a country that has a weak general will be open to attack.*

Your success in the physical world is a manifestation of your inner world (i.e., your thought and beliefs). To become successful you must learn to control your thoughts and beliefs for they create your reality.

Olivia believes that saving money impacts her sense of freedom, so she spends her money freely and shows no self control. Eventually this becomes a long-term lifestyle choice but when a challenge or an opportunity arises, she has no savings — and no freedom — to address either.

Kelly saves 10 percent of every dollar she earns. When a medical emergency or opportunity to travel abroad presents itself, she manages each with no trouble. She's earned the freedom to do this and her quality of life reflects the positive outcomes of her efforts.

Sometimes people see what they want to see. They look for and find evidence to fit their beliefs and remain blind to all other options because they refuse to even consider them. Be like the strong general and act in ways that you know will lead to success, not stress.

Sun Tzu said: *A poor general can bring misfortune upon his army in three ways:*

(1) A General who commands his army to retreat or advance, when they are not able to do so. This is called handicapping the army.

(2) When a General commands his army like his ruler governs his kingdom, when ignorant of their condition and circumstances. This causes agitation in the soldiers' minds.

(3) Commanding his officers without thinking of their situation and with ignorance of military principle. This will then shake the self-confidence of the soldiers.

Don't ask yourself or those around you to do the impossible.

Don't try to use one solution to fit all situations.

Don't repeat the same action regardless of the situation.

Don't ask your spouse to drive more quickly if you're stuck in a traffic jam.

Don't apply for a position for which you are clearly not qualified in the hopes that you will pick up the skills you need to succeed while on the job. Get the training you need before you apply to ensure your success.

Even saving money can be great in some situations but not so great in others. If you save money by eating at fast food restaurants whenever you do eat out, that's great. But if you take an important client out to eat at a fast food restaurant, that's not so great.

Don't continue buying expensive handbags or gadgets when you've just been told your pay must be cut. Keep an eye on changes within your environment and change your actions accordingly.

Don't try to sell ice to Eskimos. Don't try to sell beef burgers to vegetarians. A little common sense really does go a long way.

Sun Tzu said: *When the army is restless and lacking in unity they will be easily influenced and led astray by others. When there is a lack of unity then anarchy has a chance to seed itself and grow, thus destroying any chances of victory.*

Teamwork is a vital ingredient for success in any project or task. This is true not only in business but in most aspects of life.

Look to create a win-win situation in which all participants benefit.

Win-win situations increase your success potential

because of the positive network of opportunities they create. Those who have worked with you in any capacity and found you to be dependable and professional are much more likely to refer you for opportunities that arise in the future, some of which you otherwise may not have known existed.

Cherise wants to get a taxi to the airport but only has $20 when the fare will cost $40. It's getting pretty late and she is going to miss her flight, so she approaches some other people at a taxi stand and learns that Roberta is also in line for a cab ride to the airport. Cherise suggests Roberta share a cab with her.

During the drive Cherise mentions she's a screenwriter and Roberta remarks she knows people who invest in new films along similar lines as Cherise's current project. The women exchange contact information and plan to get in touch the following day. Not only does each save $20 on cab fare but Cherise arrives at the airport on time, Roberta arrives early, and each has expanded her professional network. Cherise may really win if this chance meeting results in a lucrative business opportunity she otherwise didn't even know existed.

In another instance you may connect a right real estate

agent with a buyer you know personally and collect a referral fee.

You may open operate a recruitment firm through which you place personnel in businesses that need that talent. You win as you earn your referral fee, the job candidate who gets the job wins as she takes another step up the corporate ladder, and the hiring company wins as they get their talented new executive.

Or you may learn of a company that makes microchips but desperately needs some cash to grow. You offer them $15 million for a 40-percent stake, a move that turns into a win-win as the company expands quickly to meet increasing demand and you get to invest before the company goes public.

Sun Tzu The Art of Making Money

Sun Tzu said: *There are five essentials for victory:*

(1) Knowing when to fight and when not to fight.

(2) Knowing how to manage superior and inferior forces and resources.

(3) Knowing how to instill strength and honor in all of your forces.

(4) Planning and preparation, and then waiting to take on the enemy when he least expects it.

(5) Acquiring enough resources and firepower for the job but also being clear about your objective.

Anyone can be successful if they follow each of these steps:

(1) Know when to take action and when to stop and change course.

(2) Know how to apply the resources you have against the situation at hand.

(3) Know how to work well with other people. Learn to be a people person.

(4) Keep learning and adding to your skill set and apply those skills in surprising ways.

(5) Gather your resources; acquire a broad range of skills, and save enough money to start your own business or to start investing. Listen to your inner calling and go full force with it.

Sun Tzu said: *If you know yourself and know your enemy then you need not fear the result of one hundred battles. If you know yourself but not the enemy then you may suffer a defeat for every victory you win. If you know neither your enemy nor yourself then you will succumb in every battle.*

Know your strengths and also your weaknesses, then play to your strengths and reduce the negative impact of your weakness. If you can master and work well with these two aspects of your being you will be much more successful in all you do.

If you don't know the area you are going into, then you

will suffer from set-backs and defeat. When this happens use each defeat to learn what will make you wiser and stronger as you gather your forces to try a new tactic.

The more you know about the terrain and the stronger your capabilities, the better your life will be.

Michael M. K. Cheung

IV. Tactical Dispositions

Sun Tzu said: *A skilled soldier puts himself beyond the possibility of defeat and then patiently waits for the right moment to strike and defeat the enemy.*

Before you engage in any venture, project, or task assess the associated risks and how to minimize them. By putting yourself beyond defeat and waiting for the chance to defeat the enemy you set yourself up for the best vantage point from which to engage.

Sun Tzu said: *Secure yourself against defeat by your own hands, but wait for the enemy to provide the opportunity for his own defeat.*

Train yourself and be prepared to take action when the ideal opportunity arises. When opportunity meets preparedness, good things happen. People often call that being lucky.

Be the change you want to see. If you want to be a manager, behave like a manager.

Read books written by other successful people, join forums and attend workshops and seminars that engage you and expand your knowledge and put you in the ranks you want to join.

Listen to motivational speakers and emulate the successful attributes they expound.

Sun Tzu said: *A skilled soldier may be able to make his position unassailable but he cannot be certain of defeating his enemy.*

You can prepare yourself to the best of your abilities and you can execute your actions flawlessly but you can never remove the possibility of defeat. There will always be outside forces that are beyond your control which will decrease your chances of success.

To maximize your chances of success regardless of such obstacles, develop and practice your technique until it's perfected.

Sun Tzu The Art of Making Money

Sun Tzu said: *A person may know how to conquer but without being able to do so when it comes to putting theory into practice.*

Even if you know an area well and can execute your plan flawlessly the environment in which you operate may not be conducive to your success.

Mark, a car designer, has designed a wonderful high-end sedan but the market shows little interest in luxury cars due to the current recession. The car also doesn't sell well due to high oil prices. For these and other related reasons that lead to low sales, Mark doesn't get the big raise he thinks he deserves.

Sandy runs a recruitment agency. She knows how to source good candidates and has great companies on her books, but the job market is so poor no one is hiring. She decides to supplement her income with a second job while she focuses on increasing her networking efforts to make sure she's part of the next big hiring push in the industry in which it occurs.

Sun Tzu said: *To prevent the enemy from defeating you, use defensive tactics; to beat the enemy go on the offensive.*

Both defensive and offensive approaches are important

and one should work to master both. In order to win, however, you have to spend at least some time playing offense. Pursuing defensive tactics only eventually drains your energy and resources while it gets you nowhere. Being on the offensive, however, furthers your progress in reaching your goals, giving you the increased energy and motivation you need to continue to press on towards victory.

Tad has always been on the defensive. He lets things happen to him rather than work to make things happen.

At work Tad plays it so safe he gets overlooked for promotions that could have landed him a job as a sales manager long ago.

Sally, meanwhile, plays great offense. She is proactive about getting into new projects as soon as her boss mentions them. She even takes the initiative to suggest new project ideas to her boss. While she gets the projects she wants because she's always willing to lead the way, Tad consistently gets saddled with the projects neither he nor anyone else wants.

Michael is a go-getter in business. He is always looking

for new markets in which to operate and new sales opportunities. His business has grown because he always leads the way. When Asian markets began to take off he took a seven-day intensive course to learn Mandarin Chinese, then flew to China to pursue new business opportunities there that immediately took off.

Bob is a defensive player and is very careful with his money, which he puts primarily into CDs and government bonds. He gets interest but much of his profit is eaten up by inflation. When the government lowers interest rates, all he can do is wait for interest rates to someday go back up. He is at the mercy of the Federal Reserve.

Rachel, on the other hand, buys stocks that are doing well in Asian markets as well as companies that benefit from lowered interest rates. She invests in real estate investment trusts and earns 20-percent interest paid monthly and quarterly. She's also bought a commodities index fund which is doing well as oil and precious metals have risen in value. She is making a good return on her money because she is proactively researching and getting into all the hot markets.

Sun Tzu said: *When you are of insufficient strength you may need to be on standby; but once you have an abundance of resources you can attack.*

When people play on the defensive they normally lack something. Ask yourself if you lack any of the following:

- Self-esteem or self-confidence
- Savings
- Energy

A shortage of any of these can impact your willingness or ability to go on the offensive and be more proactive. Identify your weaknesses in these areas and focus on improving them so you can acquire the confidence you need to effect positive change.

Frank is lacking in self-esteem and is very defensive about everything. He is socially withdrawn and very anxious around people. He lacks social skills and likes to keep to himself. He also expects little out of life. He is not very confident with his ideas and actions and tends to not follow through with anything. He lets things happen to him, and is miserable.

Betty is a confident lady and has high self-esteem. She is talkative and loves to chat and socialize all the time. She is also a great listener and when she has an idea she follows through with it as efficiently as she can. She tends to make things happen and is always getting invited to do new things.

Betty recognizes Frank's low self-esteem and tells him about classes on how to build self-confidence and encourages him to take them. She even helps him sign up for his first class and introduces him to a friend of hers who will also attend. Frank is surprised to learn at his first class that there are measured steps he can take to improve his ability to better handle social situations. Over the course of many months of classes he gains the skills to build his confidence level and finds he enjoys not only attending the classes but going out with new friends afterward.

Rick has a small business and would like to open more of his home-town hardware stores but lacks the financial resources. So he is being defensive and keeping his budget tight as he operates just one shop. If he could acquire additional funding from his bank or an investor he could go on the offensive and open more stores.

Michael M. K. Cheung

Sun Tzu said: *The general who is a master of defensive strategies will hide himself and his forces, but a general who is a master of offensive strategies will launch an attack from sea, land, or from the heavens with lighting speed and precision. A master of defensive skills will be protective and a master of offensive skills will attack. He who knows both will have ultimate victory.*

In the Chinese philosophy of Taoism the yin-yang symbol represents shadow and light. This symbol shows how polar opposites are connected. One cannot be without the other. There is day and night, hot and cold, male and female.

Yin and yang are not opposing forces, but are complementary in nature.

Defensive and offensive skills represent complementary disciplines. When you use both well, a synergetic force is created which makes you extremely powerful.

The yin-yang symbol is also symmetrical, which reflects the need for balance when using these disciplines. Too much defensive and too little offensive, or vice versa, will result in an unbalanced set of results.

George, a recent college graduate, works every waking moment on his current project at his new job. His boss loves him and his team admires him. It looks like George is off to a great start to his career.

But George has neglected to balance things, so his defensive side is weak. He hasn't eaten properly in weeks; he hasn't spoken to or seen his girlfriend in weeks, apart from the briefest of phone calls and a few texts. He also hasn't been sleeping much and is drinking tons of coffee.

George gets a big pay rise and promotion from his boss, but the next day he doesn't show up at the office. His boss calls his cell and finds out George is in hospital, recovering from exhaustion.

Remember an army marches on its stomach. Taking care of yourself is a form of defense that must be practiced on a regular basis.

Sun Tzu said: *A general who is able to win a battle when he has numerical superiority cannot consider himself elite.*

A leader's victories carry no accolades for wisdom or courage when the bar is set too low.

When you are comfortable in life you are probably not growing because you are not challenging yourself. You can only be as successful as your current levels of knowledge and skill will allow.

Michael M. K. Cheung

Look beyond your comfort level and strive for more. Take chances; set yourself goals that challenge you. When you reach one target, focus on the next level and work towards that new goal.

Hank is great at selling to small retail shops and makes an okay living doing that, but he is not hitting the top dollar because he's afraid to step out of his comfort zone. He has his routines and he likes to stick with them. Opportunities to sell to bigger corporate buyers have presented themselves in the past, but Hank has opted not to take advantage of them, despite the potential for much bigger commissions. He's convinced himself he likes to keep things simple.

Ken is great at selling preserves and other shelf-stable products from his farm to buyers in his local area. He does it well but hesitates to scale up production to try to meet increased demands from outside his immediate home base. Instead, he simply turns away business.

His wife, Theresa, however, can't stand to turn away customers so she learns what needs to be done to hire on help and renovate their production line so they can fill orders from all over. Within a year, Ken is glad she convinced him to expand their business. He's already making plans for further expansion of his now very lucrative company.

Sun Tzu said: *A general who wins his battles and is pronounced a genius is not one just because his nation calls him one. A general should be considered a genius or elite only when his actions have shown his worth.*

To pick up an autumn leaf is not a sign of great strength. To see the moon on a winter's night is not a sign of good sight. To hear the coming of a storm from the rage of thunder is not a sign of a keen ear.

Don't sell yourself short. You are capable of doing great things, things that you never have believed were possible. Look at each day and recreate it anew. Do not strive for ordinary or second best, but strive for the best within you.

At the same time, be realistic about your resources and abilities, your strengths and weaknesses, the areas in which you need to improve in order to succeed as well as the areas in which you naturally excel.

Michael M. K. Cheung

Toby used to love playing board games, especially the fantasy ones that included trolls, orcs, and dwarfs. However all his classmates thought it was a stupid waste of his time and told him to stop playing these games. Toby didn't want to seem out of place and, due to such peer pressure, stopped playing the games.

During college Toby joined a video gaming club and started to take computer design classes. Upon graduation he became a video game designer, a job he loves that allows him to draw on his old passion for games and put it and his new-found talents to good use.

Jason had always been interested in investing and from a young age read all he could about property management. His friends discouraged him for going into property investing, however, saying it was very difficult.

Jason recognized that his friends didn't share his passion for or even have an interest in real estate so he took a chance on doing what he loved. Twenty years later, he manages a property empire worth millions and has business contacts all over the world.

Sun Tzu The Art of Making Money

Sun Tzu said: *To be called the title of elite one should not only have victory but should gain it with ease.*

When a great general wins his battles due to making no mistakes then his certainty of victory is sure to follow from that. The enemy's defeat was laid as soon as the general made his position unassailable.

A skillful general makes sure he positions himself so that defeat is impossible and then looks for the first moment in which he can defeat his enemy.

You can't anticipate and compensate for every possible mistake you may make or each surprise obstacle that may appear in your way, but you can focus on taking one step at a time toward your ultimate goal.

And that requires planning. It is better to execute an average idea brilliantly than to execute a brilliant idea poorly. Be systematic and methodical in your approach at all levels.

Success is often obtained when excessive preparation leads to easy execution. Wise preparation is critical to success.

Nina has graduated from college and is looking for a job. She applies for a job as a salesperson for XYZ and Co Clothing. Before going to her interview she reads about the company, finds out what they sell and which of their products consistently sell well. She also looks up the markets in which they operate, their top competitors, and the company's history and culture.

Nina then asks her mom to conduct a mock interview with a set of interview questions from the web that relate specifically to retail.

It takes a bit of time and effort to prepare for her interview, but after three days of such a systematic and methodical approach Nina feels ready. To make sure she arrives on time, she looks up the quickest route from her home to the office in which she'll be interviewed and does a mock run to assess how long it might take and to see where she can park.

On interview day, Nina arrives early. Her 30-minute interview covers nearly everything she's learned. Not one question is asked that she can't quickly and easily answer.

Claire, on the other hand, also applied for the same job and got an interview. She did not read about the company, did no research or mock interview and failed to drive the route to the interview office the day before.

When her interview day came, Claire arrived 20 minutes late. During her interview she couldn't name the company's best-selling product or top markets. Because Claire didn't give herself the advantage of excellent planning and preparation, her execution suffered terribly.

Predictably, Claire didn't get the job but Nina did.

Paul goes that extra mile in his business. Every time one of his customers makes a comment he looks to see if he needs to make an improvement. He does this on a daily basis and often delivers product personally to make sure it arrives on time. Paul is building brand excellence. His company has won many awards for being so customer-focused.

Vick has been running his business for a while now and is used to getting customer complaints about late deliveries. Vick ignores these customers and their fussy complaints. He believes all is well and there are many more customers on the way. But Vick's customers are losing patience with him and his company and are looking for other alternatives. His main competitor, Paul, is welcoming all these customers with assurances that his company will provide the service they need.

Patrick analyzes all his stocks. He reads all the reports, goes to all the companies' annual general meetings, and even visits the places where products are sold or tries out companies' services. He leaves no stone unturned as he learns how the companies operate, make their profits, and make up for their losses.

Patrick has a phenomenal level of success with his investments because he is so focused on being successful with them.

Sun Tzu said: *A master strategist will only seek to engage in battle when victory has already been won first in the mind and he need only execute his plan. A general who is destined for defeat will fight first and analyze the situation later.*

Put all your efforts into preparation and planning. Stack the odds in your favor and only take risks and engage in things when there is a high probability of success. Identify your goal and how best to achieve it before you take action.

William has a job at an investment bank as a trader. But he didn't get there by luck. William first thought about being a trader when he was in high school. He decided the best way to become one was to learn from people who already were traders. He got his chance when his Brooklyn school did a work experience project at the New York Stock Exchange.

William spent two weeks following traders around and observing how they worked. He listened and asked questions, often reading up on the subject the night before. By doing that he maximised what he could learn from those in the know.

One of the traders, Callum, was so impressed by William that he gave him his business card at the end of the school project and invited him to visit again or consider working with him to earn a bit of extra money.

William soon called Callum and arranged to work as a runner for him over the next few summers, moving order tickets and performing other related duties.

When William graduated from college he was able to get a job quickly at an investment bank due to his experience working at the NYSE. Callum wrote a glowing recommendation for William which also helped pave the way for him.

Helen wanted to open a cake bakery-tea shop. She didn't know much about it as a business but liked to bake cakes at home. She had her weekends free so she found work at a bakery to get valuable experience of how such a business is run.

While she was working she also developed her business plan, which included her USP (Unique Selling Point). Eventually she also brought in a partner who had experience running the financial aspects of a successful small business.

Helen prepared and planned well. She stacked the odds in her favor by working in her field of interest and developing a business plan. Partnering with someone with experience running a business also left her free to focus on the creative aspects of her new company.

Rory is a great investor. He knows there are thousands of companies out there in which he could invest, but he also knows how to stack the odds in his favor. He uses the "Zulu principle" as described by investor Jim Slater in his book *The Zulu Principle: Making Extraordinary Profits from Ordinary Shares.*

The principle suggests that you succeed by becoming the expert in a narrow field of interest. Rory focuses on dividend stocks and limits his investments to companies in the oil industry, where he used to work. He built a portfolio of 15 stocks that meet his high-yield criteria and looks for those that pay between five- and ten-percent dividends.

In all these examples, the chances of victory are raised significantly by so much planning and hard work.

Sun Tzu Said: *A supreme general who follows the moral law and strictly observes method and discipline will thus be gifted the power to control success.*

Work to align your inner and outer mission and apply a systematic methodical approach to joining the two. When you fuse your inner world with your outer world you are much more likely to achieve extraordinary success.

Inner world desire: You dream of becoming a doctor.

Outer world reality: You are currently a student in school.

Consider your best inner qualities:

You are a hardworking person.

You are a caring person.

You have a scientific mind.

You have good communication skills.

Are you reflecting your inner qualities in your outer world?

Are you using and practicing them in the outer world?

Your inner world only becomes crystalized when you <u>actually do something</u> with your inner qualities. For example you may think you are a caring person but when did you last make an effort in the real world to care for someone? When did you last bring food to an elderly neighbour or ask how they are?

You may think you are a hardworking person but when was the last time you actually helped a friend move or pulled an all-night job on a project?

You may think you have a scientific mind but when did you last question the status quo and research a unique idea rather than regurgitate someone else's ideas?

You may think you have good communication skills but when was the last time you listened to someone without interrupting them? When did you last listen empathically to someone else's problems?

Thinking is the realm of the inner world but to transform that into the outer world you need to take action. Reading a book about running a business is not the same as setting up a business and experiencing all the related challenges, setbacks, frustrations, and eventually successes and joys.

To make your inner world your new reality you need to change, take action, take the first step.

Fred has dreams of becoming a public speaker and motivational trainer. His outer world currently consists of his position as a data analyst for a marketing company. Fred decided to take some evening classes on public speaking and got involved in some weekend workshops which involved his favourite hobby, paragliding.

As Fred spent more time on these extra activities he noticed that his confidence began to improve and he was more at ease with speaking in front of small groups of people. He had taken the first steps on his journey to his dream of becoming a speaker and a trainer.

Mandy has always wanted to start her own business as a women's shoe designer. She has a lot of talent and has always been good at drawing and designing things, but she is not very focused. Mandy decides to take the plunge and learn to design shoes. She takes some basic design classes and shows her designs to someone who can help make them into working prototypes. In a short time period Mandy has gone from wanting to start a business to learning about her field of interest through a low-risk strategy. She hasn't spent a lot of money or stocked up on any supplies or leased office space. She simply got directly involved in the field and is now preparing and planning to find a business partner to help her get to the next level.

Ralph was always good at numbers and analytical work but hated working in a structured environment. Ralph's inner world was made up of mathematics and formulas but he didn't like the idea of working for someone else or running a brick-and-mortar store. Ralph sold his house and car and invested the money in a course on how to buy and sell options. He went on to trade options on his laptop and now makes a living doing that. Ralph had to change by taking a course and making some personal sacrifices such as selling his home and car. Such actions, however, helped him move from dreaming about being an investor to becoming one.

Sun Tzu Said: *In method of warfare we first must consider the attribute called Measurement, then Estimation of quantity, then Calculations followed by Balancing of the chances and, finally, Victory.*

Some form of <u>measurement</u> is needed in order to assess success. In business, key performance indicators (or key success indicators) are measurements that most accurately reflect areas in which a business competes and wants to excel

Once you have decided which measure best indicates your level of success, you need to track the <u>quantity</u> of that measure. Do you consider yourself successful if you're making $50K a year, for example, or if you're making $200K a year?

<u>Calculations</u> help us remember that a task has variables that need to be considered which will affect its outcome. Such variables can include materials used in a construction project and the outcomes that will be achieved if a bridge is made of wood, brick, or steel.

<u>Balancing of chances</u> involves the understanding of the results of the calculations and the outcomes that will arise from applying different variables to the calculations.

A wooden bridge, for example, would be able to hold up 100 percent of the time when a small car crosses over it, but if a large tank were to cross it might have a 70 percent chance of collapsing.

Victory is the outcome of all these things going your way. By planning and building your bridge with materials that can withstand the pressures of the vehicles likely to cross it, your bridge will be successful.

Sun Tzu Said: *Measurement owes its existence to Earth, Estimation of quantity to Measurement, Calculation to Estimation of quantity, Balances of chances to Calculation, and Victory to Probabilities.*

Note the dependant nature of victory. Victory must be defined. Without such a definition, how does one know if he's succeeded or not?

When you define victory you bring yourself closer to it because you can make an informed judgement as to what you need to do in order to achieve it. If you just take action without understanding what victory requires, then you could be using your resources in places in which it is not helping you be successful.

Choose a measure, choose the quantity for that measure, determine what calculations produce that quantity and what chances work with your calculations, and finally understand that those outcomes reveal if victory is yours or not.

Sun Tzu Said: *A winning army compared to a failed one is like a lead weight place in the balancing scales against a single grain.*

Defeat is demoralizing and weighs upon the soul, while victory uplifts the victor and energizes him to further successes. Choose your measure of success wisely because if it truly tests you it will take much effort to achieve. When you do achieve it, however, enjoy the spoils.

Ryan decided that his success was tied to his ability to become a doctor. He worked long and hard for years and sacrificed a lot. When he did graduate as an MD, however, he felt a bit empty inside and began to wonder if he should've followed his passion for music, for which he had a natural inclination. He decided to perform in a coffee shop near the hospital during lunch breaks and became well known for his many talents.

Tina wanted to run a multimillion-dollar business that sold women's handbags. She had worked hard for ten years and had finally made it when she was invited to a business award ceremony. Tina had been voted top entrepreneur of the year for her city, and when she approached the podium to speak she was in tears—tears of joy that she had reached the pinnacle of her journey. A great victory had been won.

Julian knew he had made it as an investor when he'd built up a property empire worth millions. Even though he could afford to stop working, he didn't. Julian loved being an investor; he loved doing deals and owning properties. He had realized his childhood Monopoly dreams of owning not only one red hotel, but many.

Sun Tzu Said: *The rush of conquering forces should be likened to the bursting of water from a dam cascading down a chasm a thousand feet deep.*

When you succeed in an area for which you are destined, you feel the rush and exhilaration of being alive. Money should not be a driving force for victory—passion should be that force. Money simply provides a way to keep score of how well you are doing.

Michael M. K. Cheung

V. Energy

Sun Tzu said: *The control of a large resource requires the same principles as the control of a smaller resource; it is merely a question of dividing up their numbers.*

Success often requires that you first learn to manage a project on a small scale and then exponentially increase your efforts to build the size of that project while also increasing your skills and ability to manage things well.

Erin was in hundreds of dollars' worth of debt. Rather than manage that by cutting back on spending and slowly paying down her debt, she decided to take out a bank loan to pay it off. For a while she seemed okay but unfortunately her spending habits hadn't changed. She was still spending more than she earned and soon owed thousands of dollars. Had Erin learned how to take care of a few hundred dollars worth of debt she would have avoided the much larger problem she now faces.

Evan was running a successful business that was growing quickly. He had five staff working for him but he didn't know how to manage them and left them to their work. As his business expanded he added more and more staff until he had 100 staff working for him. Still, however, he didn't know how to manage them. What had been a small group of five people doing their own thing had become a mess of 100 team members with no direction regarding company policies or work projects.

While Evan tried to keep his company's projects on track and his clients happy he eventually also discovered all the staff were using their company credit cards to pay for parking fines and lunches and other personal expenses. These expenses added up to thousands of dollars his business was forced to pay.

If Evan had simply hired someone up front who could help him manage not only his employees' projects but put into place a simple accounting and budget system that could be scaled easily as his company grew, then he would have avoided the problems he encountered.

Sun Tzu Said: *To employ a large army is no different from using a regiment; it is a matter of instituting signals and signs.*

Establish a system through which you issue orders and

those under you follow them. A staff training manual should be equally useful whether you have one staff member or 100 staff members.

Peyton was always having trouble with her spending so she decided to put a system in place to help her manage her money better.

She first created a budget of what she needed to spend each month on rent, food, gas, clothes, etc. She then divided her wallet with sections for each type of expense. When Peyton cashed her pay check each month, she put the needed funds into each section of her wallet and put the rest of her money into her savings account. Peyton never spent more than she planned in any category once she began using her money wallet system.

Terry had been investing for a year and was making money from his dividend stocks but he didn't actually know how much he was earning. His friend Marcus, a computer expert, offered to help set up Terry's laptop with an Excel spreadsheet that would show how much money he was making from his various investments. Marcus even tied the spreadsheet into a data feed so the price of Terry's investments would also be updated every day.

Sun Tzu Said: *Use maneuvers that are direct and indirect to ensure you can withstand the brunt of an enemy's attack.*

Have more than one skill and more than one income stream.

Jake was very good at engineering and had specialized for years in an archaic programming language. When he was laid off from his job, he found he could not find any work in his specialty. He had to take months of classes before he was able to find another employer that agreed to continue his training while he worked in an entry-level position.

Stacy had a great business making and selling horse-riding saddles for her main customer, a horse-racing business. But when her one and only client was sold to a new owner who didn't renew her contract, Stacy found she had no other clients and no other skills that might help her get work. She had to close her business due to her single point of failure.

Sun Tzu The Art of Making Money

Harold's main skill was investing in property abroad, especially European holiday homes. He made a good income via rentals of such homes until the

European credit crunch hit. When he became unable to rent his homes, he had to sell them to keep afloat.

Sun Tzu said: *The bearing of your army may be likened to that of dashing an egg against the grind stone–you must study the science of strong and weak points in all its forms.*

Try breaking an egg by squeezing it in the palm of your hand; it is extremely difficult to break one this way. However if you hit the egg on the side with the edge of a spoon then it will break quite easily.

Apply your resources where there are weak points and avoid the strong points.

Know where to apply your skills for the best result.

Stefan has always been talented at mathematics. When he graduated from college he joined an investment bank as a quantitative analyst building complex financial trading models.

Robert was always good with speaking to people and had great communications skills but hated the structure of a corporate environment. He left the corporate world and started his own business. Robert now works as a motivational speaker helping people achieve their dreams of starting their own businesses.

Sonya was always good at numbers and art but couldn't seem to find a job that would let her shine in both fields. She decided to become a property investor and was soon buying houses at auction and fixing them up by redesigning their interiors. Sonya would then sell the homes at a high profit to young affluent couples who had no time to decorate but loved the look of her designs.

Sun Tzu said: *A general can use a direct approach to enter into battle but if he wants to gain victory he must also know how to use an indirect approach.*

You will always have a key strength in life but to be truly successful you need to develop additional skills as well.

Bruce was very good at dancing but he wasn't making

much progress at his career in the performing arts. His friend Rachel encouraged Bruce to try some singing lessons too. Bruce worked to bring his singing skills to a level at which he could use them along with his dance skills. Bruce now gets regular work in theatres and musicals as a lead male performer, whereas before he was just getting a few dance parts.

Lucinda was making dresses for weddings and was having some moderate success but she was not making the headway she wanted. Lucinda's friend Jessica asked her to come to some evening classes in making jewelery using Swarovski crystals. Lucinda found she really liked making jewelery and was actually pretty good at it. Lucinda decided to combine her knowledge of making jewelery with her dress-making skills. While her dresses had always had shape and form, after adding her new-found decorative skills to her dresses, Lucinda found what she was looking for. Her wedding dresses now looked elegant and had sparkle! And her business took off.

Neil was an investor mainly dealing with blue chip stocks; he was making okay money but was not really making the progress he really wanted. Neil's friend Don asked Neil if he wanted to take part in a sport science project in which he was already involved.

Neil had always loved science at school and had some free time so he got involved with Don's project. Neil soon realized he was really passionate about sport science and applied that into his dealings as an investor. Neil now works with a number of small companies that develop products using sports science. He has tripled his profits and loves every minute of being an active investor with those companies.

Sun Tzu said: *Indirect tactics can be used in limitless ways. They are as numerous as the stars in the night sky and they are always renewing themselves like the change of the seasons.*

Ways to make additional income are unending and ever-changing.

While dividend stocks are currently in favor, for example, a few years ago it was all about tech stocks. But before tech stocks rocketed people used to invest in growth stocks.

Money cycles constantly change and yet constantly renew themselves.

Consider the gold rushes of the 1800s, an old-fashioned type of money cycle:

1800 The North Carolina gold rush starts

1828 The Georgia gold rush starts

1848 The California gold rush starts

1858 The Colorado gold rush starts

1867 The Wyoming gold rush starts

1884 The North Dakota gold rush starts

1890 The Idaho gold rush starts

1892 The Montana gold rush starts

1898 The Alaska gold rush starts

Notice how each individual golf rush is separated by a certain number of years that usually range from about 10 to 20. The gold rush was repeated over and over in this 100-year-span, with a lot of people also making money from selling the tools, buckets, food, and beers that gold rush enthusiasts needed to keep them going.

Even today the gold rush has returned; it's simply morphed into the online trading of gold shares via digital platforms. Software vendors are the new providers of the pickaxes and buckets.

Money cycles repeat throughout history, creating and fulfilling the same needs and wants but in a slightly different way and on a slightly different playing field each time. The age of physical gold has evolved into the age of paper gold contracts.

Watch and learn from the economic and financial cycles and take advantage of them of when things come back into favor. History can teach you a lot about how to be profitable in the future.

Mark had studied the industrial revolution that happened in Great Britain at school for his school history project and noted something similar was occurring in the United States when he graduated from high school in the early 1980s. Mark decided to get in on the new trend and enrolled into a computer science course at college. When he graduated, he was positioned to take advantage of the computer revolution that by then was in full swing.

Brendan had read about the property boom in the UK that had occurred in the late 1980s and was starting to see signs of that happening again in the UK twenty years later. Brendan had noticed that sometimes it takes about twenty years before people have had enough time to forget about the bust time for a new boom to begin. Brendan started buying investment properties in the UK in the early 2000s, when prices were low. He sold most of his property eight years later and made phenomenal gains. Brendan is now on the lookout for other business cycles that he can capitalize on by studying historic records.

Sun Tzu said: *There are no more than five musical notes, yet the world is filled with more music that you can ever listen to in your lifetime.*

There are only five primary colors (red, blue, yellow, black, and white) but when combined they create an infinite number of colors, more than can ever been imagined.

There are not more than five basic tastes (salt, sweet, acrid, sour, and bitter) but when combine they create more flavors than a chef could ever dream of.

Simply collecting more and more skills will not make you successful due to the law of diminishing returns. How you use what you know is what matters.

For example, if you have one skill and then you gain a new one you have acquired a big gain in your potential. Say you double your chances of success. Adding a third skill, however, gives you a 33-percent extra benefit, while adding a fourth skill may give you a 25-percent extra benefit. Finally, adding a fifth skill might get you a 20-percent extra gain. The benefit gained from adding more skills eventually grows smaller.

Master a limited number of key skills and then apply them well. That is a key secret to success.

A computer has five basic instructions, to add, subtract, branch, store, and retrieve. Every amazing thing you see a computer do is built around those five basic instructions or skills. You might be playing a really cool 3D game like Halo and, believe it or not, every aspect of it is driven by those five basic instructions applied in complex and amazing ways.

The programmers who wrote Halo were able to apply

those instructions at a very high level with a high degree of expertise, precision, and knowledge. In this way mastery of the basic skills and their applications can yield extraordinary results, limited only by your imagination.

A lot of people get caught up in wanting to acquire more skills or learn more things, hoping to uncover a secret gold mine along the way.

Instead, look within yourself and remember that part of the key to your success lies within you. It is your self-belief that grants you victory. You cannot have success without doing something and applying yourself, and none of that is possible without self-belief.

Sun Tzu said: *There are only two styles of attack in battle, that is the indirect and the direct; when these two are arrangement they give rise to an unending series of maneuvers.*

The indirect and the direct follow each other in turn. It is like the turning of a wheel - It never comes to an end. Can anyone exhaust the possibilities of their combinations?

By applying all the different skills that you have, you can produce an endless series of results. Look to your own inner well of strength and apply those skills when you are faced with each new challenging situation. As long as you have hope you always have the chance for victory. The chance for victory is only lost when you give up hope.

Sun Tzu said: *When the army forces are released into battle it is likened to the torrent of water rushing down a mountain during a storm; even stone, mud, and wooden stumps are washed along it course.*

When you begin any task there is always resistance, be it

from yourself (an internal resistance) or from others (an external resistance). To be successful you must exert enough energy to break through such resistance. Once you have done that then the boulder that has been blocking your path begins to move slowly. To create a torrent of force you must keep that initial momentum moving by applying energy at a consistent level over a period of time.

It is better to apply a consistent small amount of energy over a long period of time than it is to apply a huge amount of energy over a short period of time.

Which person will move the boulder farthest? The person who exerts a consistent force over a larger period of time.

Sun Tzu said: *The quality of decision is like the well-timed swoop of an eagle which enables it to accurately strike and kill its victim.*

Focus your energies and make sure they are having the desired effect. Don't put out a lot of energy in an unfocused way. Conserve your energy and direct it in short but effective bursts.

There is not a linear relationship between the effort used and the results produced. Doubling you effort doesn't always result in doubling your success level.

A principle known as the Pareto principle, also known as the 80-20 rule, states that about 80 percent of effect comes from 20 percent of cause.

Successful people either consciously or subconsciously apply this principle though various aspect of their lives. They maximize their efforts in the 20 percent area which then produces the 80-percent result they want. Successful people are not looking for perfection or 100-percent results. They are looking to maximize their results by expending the least amount of resources. That is not to say that they don't put effort into going that extra mile. Rather, it means they <u>focus</u> their efforts and put in that extra mile in the 20-percent area that will deliver the 80-percent result so their chance of success is increased.

Sun Tzu said: *A good general will be slow at the beginning while circling his enemy, probing for weaknesses, but when striking he will be quick and accurate like the eagle.*

While assessing a situation take your time to plot your best course, but once you've committed waste no time in taking action. Move swiftly and execute without second thoughts or hesitation.

Sun Tzu said: *Energy can be likened to the bending of a crossbow; decision, to the releasing of a trigger.*

Change is instant, like the releasing of a trigger.

The bending of a crossbow holds the energy required to move all obstacles out of the way so you are put in a position ready for change.

This energy is the mental preparation work or groundwork you do to put you in that state of readiness. The key, then, is to be in the correct mental state when it is time to release that energy and take action.

To clear away any confusion or denial or any other distraction that can block your chances for success, consider researching different types of psychotherapy than can help you understand and better control your mind-body connections.

Some people have found success with an approach known as neuro-linguistic programming (NLP), which can help one recognize what's blocking their efforts and get "unstuck" so they can instantly act and succeed. Replacing fear with images of a successful mentor in action can help you feel more confident, especially if you've spent a lot of time researching that person and his methods.

Sun Tzu said: *In the heat of the battle there may seem to be disorder where there is in fact a plan. Among the chaos and confusion there is method to what appears to be madness.*

Sometimes you may feel many things are occurring at the same time and you are not making any progress. Especially at such trying times, keep in mind the big picture of your ultimate goal, even as you struggle to cope with a seemingly endless stream of small challenges.

Think of Thomas Edison, who endured hundreds of failed attempts before he finally got a light bulb to work correctly.

Think of Henry Ford, who made numerous attempts until he finally produced an automobile that was within the economic reach of the average American.

Keep the faith, the vision, and the big picture in mind as you continue with determination to overcome your obstacles and see your project through to its completion.

Sun Tzu said:

To successfully simulate disorder to confuse your enemy, you must have perfect discipline.

To simulate fear among your soldiers to entrap your enemy, you must have courage.

To simulate weakness to make your enemy arrogant, you must have much strength.

It takes great discipline, courage, and strength to deceive and overcome your enemy, whatever form it takes.

To become disciplined, put energy into being structured and organized in all aspects of your life.

To gain courage, face your fears and do courageous things to help you overcome them.

To gain strength, identify one of your weaknesses, whether it's physical or mental, and take small steps to improve it over a long period of time. Develop a plan to do this and stick to it.

Sun Tzu said: *The clever fighter uses the power of combined energies and does not depend solely on the exceptional skills of any individual. He picks out the right people and teaches them to work together to create a greater effect.*

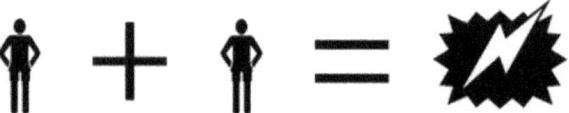

Being successful does not have to be an individual affair. You can achieve an even greater victory when you use the effort of many.

Carol understood that her business could not achieve its full potential if she tried to do it all. So she hired an accountant to help with the numbers, a delivery man to move product to the customer, a secretary to field customers' calls, and an IT guy to look after the website. By assembling a great team with their own unique talents she was able to grow her business and achieve the success she sought.

Sun Tzu Said: *When a clever fighter uses the power of combined energy he can create a cohesive force that is like drops of rain falling on the leaves of a tree seemingly gentle and, when collected in force, able to smash trees and rocks. When it becomes a torrent, such a force can burst through a swollen river bank and destroy everything in its path.*

A team must have a clearly stated goal or mission before it can unleash its full power to great effect.

Lucy wanted to build a house and hired an architect to draw up plans but she kept changing her mind on what she wanted. Every time she read a new article she wanted to try a new idea out on her house. First it was going to be an eco-friendly solar-paneled house and then it was going to be a cottage with old wood shutters, and then she wanted it to be a modern glass building or a 1920 English country manor.

Her poor architect would start and get so far and then keep on changing the plan to incorporate her new ideas. He was talented and wanted to work with Lucy but could not because her goals kept changing. Had Lucy been clear on what she wanted her architect would have designed a fantastic house for her.

Ray was running a restaurant. He first told his staff it was going to be a pizza place since he'd styled it and decorated it that way. His team had designed some nice menus and the chef had put together a wonderful pizza menu. Ray then fell in love with the idea of having a fresh fish restaurant and so he got his chef to change the menu to one that served primarily seafood. Soon Ray wanted to change from being a fish restaurant to one that was a steak house. Finally, Ray's staff and customers were confused and no one knew what the restaurant was about. Ray lost customers and staff and had to close his business.

Sean told his broker he wanted to invest in precious metals but didn't say how to do it. So his broker bought him shares in a gold mining company called Gold World XYZ Corp. Soon gold went up $100 an ounce and Sean called his broker to ask him how much money he had made.

Sean was down $10K. He was furious and asked how that could be possible. His broker explained that he'd followed Sean's instructions and bought shares in a gold mining company that then had lost money when two of its mines were flooded. Even though gold had gone up $100 an ounce the company lost money.

Sean argued he'd said to buy into gold. His broker said he did. Sean said he meant gold as in gold coins or gold bars.

His broker insisted Sean had never given an order to buy gold bars but had said he wanted to get into precious metals. The broker bought what he'd thought was the best play on precious metals for Sean.

Sean hadn't been clear about what he wanted, and his broker had done his best by buying into a gold mining company.

Sun Tzu Said: *The energy developed by the cohesion of a united force can move trees and mountains. Such is the force of nature and unity.*

A set of skilled people working together to achieve a clear objective can do phenomenal things. Examples of this include the building of the pyramids, or NASA putting a man on the moon or a rover on Mars.

VI. Weak Points and Strong

Sun Tzu said: *When an army is first to the battlefield it will be fresh and ready for fighting. The army that comes second will rush to get into place and will be exhausted.*

Before you take on a new task or project, make sure you set yourself up to be successful at it.

Stay alert by relaxing and sleeping well.

Strengthen your body by eating well and exercising.

Strengthen your mind and spirit by reading motivational books and biographies of successful people. Listen to motivational speakers each morning.

Plan well and be prepared for the next step on your journey.

Michael M. K. Cheung

Sun Tzu said: *A clever fighter will put his will onto his enemy but will not allow the enemy to do the same to him.*

It is not necessary to fight every battle that comes your way. Fight only the battles you can win on your terms.

Pass up or retreat from a situation that is not favorable. Choose your battles.

Larry was always of slight physical build and poor at sports, but he was always good at talking and making people laugh. Larry didn't try out for sports and instead made his way through college by being the funny guy. His personality got him all the attention he needed.

Ted couldn't compete with the chain fast food joints in his hometown but he could still succeed by selling his homemade baked authentic pizzas.

Janet couldn't compete with the large venture capital firms that poured millions of dollars into new technology start-ups, so she focused her efforts on providing investment capital and a hands-on approach to small boutique businesses run by individual fashion designers.

Sun Tzu Said: *When marching through a territory that has no enemy the soldiers will be able to move great distances without any problems.*

Keep an eye out for new and unexplored markets or opportunities and step in to fill a need the same way so many famous pioneers and innovators have done in the past.

Then consider the self-belief those pioneers and innovators needed to be successful.

Moving through uncharted territory requires immense self-belief because there are no sign posts and no one to follow. But the best opportunities can be found in such territory, and its lack of limits allows much distance to be covered at a very fast pace.

Sun Tzu said: *If you attack places that are undefended then you can be sure of victory and success. Likewise you would be wise to build your defenses so they are in an unassailable position.*

The world is always evolving and presenting new opportunities and frontiers. It is the ability to take on those undefined areas that provide us with a rich reward.

Sun Tzu said: *The art of war requires knowledge of subtlety and secrecy; if you can master these skills then the enemy's fate is in your hands.*

When you first find these new and unexplored places, your first instinct may be to rush off excited and tell everyone you know about your new find. Keep your ideas under wraps. Patent them and draw up a business plan. Take the next steps you need to make your dream a reality.

Sun Tzu: *If you target and strike at the enemy's weak points then you will be able to gain a great victory, and if you are swifter than him then you will always be out of harm's way.*

Sometimes the best way to get the most out of a new idea is to move quickly with it. If you spot a gap in the market then you have to move quickly in order to capitalize on it before others do.

The difference between moving quickly and moving slowly can be measured in the cost of millions of dollars of lost revenue or in ultimate victory.

Sun Tzu The Art of Making Money

Sun Tzu said: *If we are trying to avoid engaging in battle then we must look to put something unusual and peculiar in the enemy's way. This will make him stop and question the battlefield and this new variable.*

The art of bluffing is one of the most useful skills that one can have. It is so useful even Mother Nature uses it. The puffer fish has a slow locomotion but compensates with blowing itself up and making itself appear several times bigger while also becoming a spiky ball. This is to warn off others, but should another creature call a puffer fish's bluff it will find the spiky ball contains a toxin that can kill.

Bluffing can be a wonderful tool to get you out of a very tricky spot. When used correctly it can give you a significant advantage either in your personal, business, or investment life. But it's a skill that has to be practiced to perfection as it only works well when done well.

Sun Tzu said: *If we are able to create a cohesive force, while we cause the enemy to split up we will be able to conquer him.*

Divide and conquer. No matter how big or powerful a system is when divided it can be easily overcome. Consider a system's weakest link and attack it. Even a seemingly unbreakable force can be damaged via such a strategy.

Sun Tzu said: *We should keep the time and location of the engagement hidden from the enemy. This will mean the enemy will need to divide his force across several fronts. This will mean he is thinly spread across his borders.*

Plans that remain secret will be extremely effective as you will be able to keep your enemy guessing your next move. This will also give you time to think about your own strategy.

Manage your information flow well. The more you know about your competitors' plans the greater the advantage you have over them. The less you know about them then the lower the chance you have of success if you attack them.

Guard your own information as it can mean the difference between your competitor challenging you or leaving you alone while he tries to predict your next move.

Sun Tzu Said: *Probe the opposing force for its strengths and weaknesses. Then look at your own strengths and weaknesses and compare the two.*

Gauge your strengths and weaknesses against the task at hand.

The balance of victory is not an absolute but is a relative measure. What works in one situation may not work in another; there is no one solution fits all.

Sun Tzu Said: *Everyone can see results and how the battle was won but none can see the strategy out of which victory is evolved.*

Some successful people are like ducks that look calm and collected as they float majestically on a lake. But if you were to look underneath the surface you would see their little legs paddling furiously to keep them moving.

You do not need to show people your plans and brag about how many hours you have toiled. Just keep moving.

Sun Tzu said: *Do not reuse the same tactics which has won one victory, but instead look to varying them accordingly.*

You cannot expect to always use the same skill or strategy through life because the world is always changing. You are better off if you keep moving and going onto bigger and better things.

Take on situations and tasks on your own terms rather than someone else's. Don't let market forces or other people push you around.

Stay in flux and take on new projects and tasks when they suit you, i.e., when things are most favorable for you to be successful.

Sun Tzu said: *Strategic tactics are like water, which runs from high places to low places. Avoid what is strong; you should strike at what is weak.*

Take the path of least resistance as you remain focused on your goal, not on various problems you encounter along the way. Deal with those problems effectively and move on.

Sun Tzu The Art of Making Money

Sun Tzu said: *Just as water is in no constant shape, so in warfare there are no constant conditions. Modify your tactics in relation to your enemy.*

By focusing on the goal and looking for solutions you can find ways to reach your goal given the resources that you have. Sometimes the solution is sitting in front of you but if you don't place your awareness in that direction, you won't see it as the way forward.

Remain aware that the conditions in which you work are constantly changing and adapt your tactics accordingly. Keep learning and upgrading your skills to meet the needs of the marketplace.

Sun Tzu said: *The five elements (water, fire, wood, metal, earth) are not found in equal measure; like the changing seasons each one will have its turn to be predominant. There are hot days and cold days and the moon has it cycles.*

Everyone has a different set of personal attributes. While some people are physically strong, others are smart with numbers and others are musical and others insightful.

Some people start with more money, better connections, and in better communities with better resources such as transportation, schools, and jobs.

We all, however, have been given the gift of self-determination–we can choose to make the most of what we have and work towards being successful in whatever we do.

VII. Maneuvering

Sun Tzu said: *The general at war receives his commands from the sovereign.*

Your beliefs and passions power your feelings, which lead you to take actions toward success.

Sun Tzu said: *If you look to equip you soldiers with full gear and set to march to obtain an advantage then you may be too late, having wasted much time in getting ready. However if you are swift and send out a light response unit then you may get an advantage but at the expense of providing little food and provisions for the response team.*

Preparation does not require perfection. Act as soon as you are ready.

Sun Tzu said: *Even if you have loyal men who march on orders at double speed to cover more ground, covering a large distance in a short time to help secure you an advantage, you may find that ultimately they will be captured by the enemy as fatigue sets in.*

While a journey of a thousand miles begins with a single step it is also a marathon and not a sprint. Pace yourself for the long haul so you can maintain the strength you need to reach your goal. Use your intelligence and planning so you can finish and have that victory. Don't set yourself up to fail due to mental, physical, or financial exhaustion.

Plan your journey so you have enough resources to finish the race.

Sun Tzu said: *Place your best men in front and let weary souls trail behind and this plan will deliver just 10 percent of your forces to the chosen destination.*

March 50 miles to outflank the enemy and you may find your leader might die of exhaustion and only 50 percent of your forces reach their target.

March 30 miles to reach the same target then 66 percent of your forces will arrive intact.

By trying too hard to reach your goals you may find that your efforts will be counter-productive.

The probability of success is reduced if you try too hard with too few resources or you try to push too hard for too long. There is an art to reacting to a situation and applying the right pace so you get things done as quickly as possible but without suffering burnout.

Sun Tzu said: *If you move your armed forces without supply wagons then all is lost; if you have no food and water then all is lost; without a base to resupply your forces all is lost.*

You may arrive at your destination victorious, but at what cost?

Winning at any cost is not always ideal. What's most important is to achieve success through planning, strategy, and maneuvering so you still have your physical health, your mental health, and your financial health at the end and can enjoy your victory.

Sun Tzu said: *Don't enter in alliances until you know others' agendas.*

Entering into alliances with those whose skills vary from your own can be very advantageous and can result in outcomes that are much more successful than you could otherwise hope for.

Take time to find out as much as you can about your potential partners in any undertaking before you join in with them. Take care and do your due diligence to make sure they are trustworthy. Consider their motives and how they will benefit from working with you, as well as how you can protect yourself if things don't work out.

Sun Tzu said: *Do not enter territories unless you know its dangers and the tricks and traps that await you.*

Learn as much as you can about the terrain of the area you're entering. Be aware of potential risks and prepared to protect yourself from them.

Sun Tzu said: *When in a foreign land you should look to leverage the knowledge of local guides if you wish to take advantage of the local terrain.*

Seek out the help of guides when entering new territories. Learn from the expertise of others.

Invest in such guidance as needed. Hire the best in the business to help you get your newest venture off the ground, or the best fund manager to look after your money.

Sun Tzu said: *The decision to concentrate or divide forces must be based on the situation at hand.*

Observe the world around you and be proactive by taking advantage of opportunities as they arise from changing circumstances. Learn and be prepared to apply risk management strategies to keep you in a safe position even in the face of a widespread disaster.

Sun Tzu said: *Be as swift as the morning wind, and as impenetrable as the forest trees. When attacking and raiding move like a forest fire and when on defense be like a rocky mountain.*

Move quickly when opportunities present themselves or when danger arises, but don't take unnecessary risks.

Sun Tzu said: *When you loot the enemy be sure to divide the spoils among your soldiers and when you have gained new lands be sure to share out fairly to your men.*

Keep the gears of success moving smoothly by rewarding everyone involved in each of your victories. Create as many win-win scenarios as possible.

Sun Tzu said: *Think and consider before you take action.*

Consider your resources and all other variables such as terrain and timing before you take your first step.

Michael M. K. Cheung

Sun Tzu said: *Learn the artifice of deviation. That is the art of maneuvering.*

Continuously enhance maneuverability and resources by building up savings, cultivating relationships, and learning new skills.

VIII. Variation in Tactics

Sun Tzu said: *When you enter a difficult country, do not rest and bed in. When you are on high ground shared by others look to create alliances with them. Avoid dangerous isolated positions. When you are hemmed in, use strategy. When all else fails and you are in a desperate position then and only then you must fight.*

Do not rest on the assumptions that strategies for success that have worked in the past will continue to work despite the rapidly changing face of the economy. Simple, straightforward approaches that predicted a comfortable retirement due to decades with a single company after graduation from a good school no longer cut it. Good grades don't guarantee a job when jobs are scarce. Most people now move from company to company for various reasons rather than stay in one job for years, hoping their pension or 401K plan will be help them retire wealthy. For most, this is only a dream.

Use a multi-faceted approach through which you apply tactics unique to your situation dynamically as needed. Remain very fluid, open to take advantage of opportunities as they arise. When things get risky, join trusted alliances. Avoid dangerous and isolated positions. When you feel hemmed in, strategize a way out. And when all else fails, meet the situation head on and use all the resources you've gathered along the way to land on your feet.

Sun Tzu said: *There are some roads you must not travel and some enemies you must not engage, there are cities you must not beseige and positions you must not contest. And there are commands that must not be followed.*

Just because you can doesn't mean you should. Every child who tastes a favorite treat for the first time wants more. They want to eat it instead of dinner and eat it seven days a week. But most children are limited from indulging constantly in their favorite treats because such actions will lead them to become unhealthy.

Think before you act rather than working from impulse to satisfy each and every one of your desires. Use method and discipline to keep yourself healthy.

Sun Tzu said: *The general who is well versed with a variety of tactics will be able to take advantage of a given situation and use the resources and men at his disposal.*

Learn to balance your actions against the results you are trying to achieve. Budget your finances, for example, so you spend less than you earn and fund your savings.

Sun Tzu said: *A leader may know his country well but if he does not understand these tactics he will not be able to execute his plan effectively.*

Not only know how to put together a budget but learn how to stay within that budget.

Understand why you must do something so you have the conviction you need to carry out the task that is required. If you understand that spending more than you earn over a long period of time will mean you will get deep in debt, lose anything you've purchased, and have to work very hard for many years before you can use any of your earnings as you'd like, you're less likely to get into such a difficult position in the first place. Only once you understand such reasoning can you take steps to spend less and save more.

Sun Tzu said: *A student of war who is not well versed in how to vary his tactics and plan will fail to make full use of his resources and men, even though he may know of the five advantages.*

You may understand the five basic elements of success:

(1) Follow your passion

(2) Follow the world economic cycles

(3) Learn to navigate those economic cycles

(4) Understand you alone are in charge and responsible for your life

(5) Follow the pyramid of wealth

And you may have decided to follow the pyramid of wealth step-by-step as you develop your plan to reach financial freedom. But you also must learn to vary your plan accordingly as needed, to be less rigid so you can move like water along a path of least resistance. In this way you will expend less energy and encounter fewer dangers, thereby making the entire process much easier on yourself and those around you and your overall success much more likely.

Don't be like a billboard, stiff and inflexible, snapping in half when enough force is applied. Be like a branch on a tree that is supple and survives even the strongest of winds because it's flexible and bends as needed.

Sun Tzu said: *A wise general will look at the pros and cons and blend them to form a workable plan.*

Part of your planning must include an assessment of the pros and cons of any given situation. Often life is played on a continuum on which there are right times to attack and right times to retreat.

Consider how some advantages are worth more than some disadvantages and vice versa. They are not equal in their cause and effect.

Say you want to buy a lottery ticket. The immediate advantage of buying a ticket is that it will give you a small but distinct chance of winning a jackpot, but the disadvantage is that you have to spend $1 to buy it. Now if you can afford to lose $1 without it affecting your life in any major way then this is a small price to pay for getting a chance to win a lot of money.

The chance of winning may be very small, but the advantage of winning versus the disadvantage of losing needs to be considered before you buy the ticket.

Winning – You would win a large amount of money

Losing - You would be out $1

Now you must also consider another factor. What if that $1 is your only dollar in your pocket and if you spend it on that ticket you will have to walk five miles home rather than take the bus?

Winning – You would win a large amount of money

Losing - You would be out $1 and would need to walk home

Now you also consider another factor. What if it's the middle of the night and that $1 is the only dollar in your pocket and if you spend it on that ticket you will have to walk five miles home through a very dangerous part of town?

Winning – You would win a large amount of money

Losing - You would be out $1 and would risk getting mugged while you walked through a very dangerous part of town in the middle of the night.

Vary your plan depending on the situation.

Sun Tzu said: *Even if not all the variables are to our liking we may still have a workable plan that we can use to reach our target.*

Some setbacks are worth taking because their potential advantages outweigh their likely disadvantages.

You might cut out taking a vacation for five years, for example, because you want to save enough money so you can start a business and leave your boring job. You are going to have to suffer a bit by not taking those vacations, but you will be in a much stronger position if you don't have to borrow from your bank to start your business.

Sun Tzu said: *When we are faced with difficulties we can still win if we put to good use the advantages and opportunities do present themselves.*

When life gives you lemons, make lemonade.

Maintain a positive attitude when challenges arise so you remain open to any opportunities that may arise as a result.

For example, when one farmer noticed that oil prices were going higher he saw the good side of this and decided to grow corn and sugar cane to sell as bio fuel. Meanwhile, other farmers continued with their old ways, making much lower profits due to the cost of running their equipment. The wise farmer's business, of course, flourished because he'd remained open to the possibility that a troublesome challenge might reveal a new path to success.

Sun Tzu said: *In the art of war we must not expect that the enemy will not come but we must prepare ourselves for his arrival by making our position unassailable.*

Sun Tzu The Art of Making Money

Welcome change; a changing world creates opportunities. Be prepared and ready to grab hold of Lady Luck when she comes passing through town. Make your positions unassailable by carefully managing your resources during boom times and diligently building your cash reserves, acquiring new assets, and continuously learning new skills and knowledge. When the economic tides turn, as they will, you will have a lifeboat that will float you to safety.

Sun Tzu said: *A leader can be affected by any one of five dangerous faults:*

(1) Recklessness, which often leads to destruction;

(2) cowardice, which can lead to being captured;

(3) a hasty temperament, which can be easily provoked;

(4) a thin skin, which is highly sensitive to shame;

(5) sentimentality, which exposes him to feelings of worry and endless troubles.

These five sins can be the ruin of a great general and can occur once he is at war.

(1) Being reckless can lead to one's own demise. Think first and act later rather than try to recover from a bad situation because you couldn't be bothered to think it through before you entered it. Guard against being reckless.

(2) Being a coward can lead to one's own demise. Rather than make excuses and procrastinate and miss out on opportunities when they come along, take action and seize the day.

(3) A hasty temper or lack of emotional control can lead to one's own demise. Refuse to be easily provoked so you can avoid making thoughtless mistakes and potentially dangerous decisions.

Refuse to be manipulated in any way. Work to acquire inner peace and a Zen-like control over your emotions.

(4) Being thin-skinned can lead one to be overly sensitive to challenges or insults and act recklessly as a result. Such a person may get into a physical fight, or in a car chase, or enter into a dubious financial arrangement.

Develop a thick skin so criticism and insults wash over you. Refuse to get dragged into a bad situation. This will help you keep your weaknesses hidden and under your own control.

(5) Being too worried about those around you can cause you to make mistakes. If your focus is divided among too many places and not focused on the objective at hand then you can end up doing no one a favor.

Focus on your objective even if that means others have to sit and wait. Prioritize your time and efforts so what is most important gets done before you turn your attention to other less pressing matters.

A meeting with a foreign business associate worth $50 million should get top priority, whereas attending a Little League game with your son may have to wait until next time.

It doesn't benefit your family if you lose the deal and your job because you went to a game and missed an important meeting.

Don't try to please everyone; it's impossible.

Sun Tzu said: *When the general is killed and the army has been crushed the reason will be found in one of the five dangerous sins. Let us make these findings a matter of inquiry for our minds.*

Master the five areas so you can avoid their pitfalls.

IX. The Army on the March

Sun Tzu said: *When we are looking to bed in and create a base camp we should look first to see any sign of the enemy. We should travel over mountains as quickly as possible and stay close to green valleys.*

Find easy access to the resources you need to be successful. Opt to live in an area with the services you need and a reasonable commuting distance to your work. Locate your business in an area that makes sense.

Sun Tzu said: *Take the high ground and the well lit location.*

The high ground provides a strategic advantage. Achieving high ground can be as simple as moving up to the desk with the best view of others in your open-plan office or as complex as actively networking over decades so you come to understand the big players in your field and how they operate, and make sure they're on your side.

Sun Tzu said: *Take care of your resources and men and build your base camp on hard ground. This will ensure that your* *men are free from diseases of all kinds and will ensure you have the best chance for victory.*

Disease may come in many forms: physical disease, mental disease, social disease, or even financial disease.

Physical disease can be caused by working in a job that requires you to interact with dangerous materials, move or lift heavy objects, or get too little rest.

Mental disease can arise if you live in a neighborhood with a high crime rate or are abused by someone in any way. Discrimination or intimidation at work can lead to mental disease.

Social disease can strike when you surround yourself with negative friends and office colleagues, especially those who discourage you from taking steps toward positive change in your life.

Financial disease can occur when your home is too expensive relative to your income. If you earn $1000 a month but pay $1200 on rent, you've got a financial disease that will soon put you into a lot of debt.

Sun Tzu The Art of Making Money

Sun Tzu said: *When you are on a hill or a bank keep on the sunny side with the slope at your back. This will provide you with a good tactical position.*

Utilize the natural advantage of the ground. If you put in years of effort to get into an Ivy League school, take advantage of the many opportunities that come with being enrolled in such a prestigious university.

Sun Tzu said: *If it has been raining and the river you wish to cross is swollen wait until the water subsides.*

When the economy is not running smoothly, keep your reserves at the ready until things calm down and you can see what is actually happening.

Sun Tzu said: *Terrain that has steep dangerous cliffs, hollows and confined places with branches and thickets should be left immediately or avoided altogether.*

Put checks into place to prevent missteps.

Don't mix business with pleasure.

Avoid taking on a business partner who is a friend or borrowing from friends and family. If you have to, make them aware up front of the risk that goes with investing with you. Be honest, tell them what the money is for, and show them how it will be used in the business as though you are talking to your bank manager.

When negotiating with other business parties always have a trusted lawyer help with your negotiations. This helps keep the whole process objective and prevents you from setting yourself up for a fall.

When engaging in a new activity always give yourself a day to think about it. Don't sign on the dotted line until you've talked to a trusted resource with relevant expertise such as your lawyer.

Build a check list of things to review with the other party and your lawyer to help you avoid traps. This list might include points such as:

How long is the cooling off period? Seven days? Fourteen days? (Find out and don't be shy!)

What penalties are there for exiting early?

How exactly do you exit the product, service, or contract?

Whom do you contact if you want to get out of buying that product, service, or contract?

How is the other side making their money?

Can you negotiate a favorable exit clause on the contract before you sign?

Get a copy of the contract to read before you sign and get a copy to your lawyer for his feedback. Make sure you get it to a legal person who has the relevant expertise for that contract.

See if you can make your contract subject to x, y, z conditions which favor you (e.g., the contract is subject to being counter-signed by your company secretary or director, etc.).

Check to see what clauses favor the other side and what termination clauses they can use to exit or to prevent you from exiting.

If the other party starts to get uneasy with your questions be sure to ask them why until you fully understand their concerns.

Once you have signed or otherwise entered into a contract it can be very difficult to extricate yourself from it. It is far better to be proactive and filter out any tricks or traps before you sign. This strategy is a lot more cost-effective than paying your lawyer to fight a lengthy legal battle down the line.

Sun Tzu said: *If you find it easy to reach the enemy base camp with little resistance then it is a trap and he is lying in wait for you.*

Sun Tzu The Art of Making Money

If it sounds too good to be true then it probably is.

Such an opportunity is usually some sort of a trap and if you fall for it you may find that your investment money goes to money heaven while your overall health and positive attitude deteriorate.

There are people out there who make a living from being conmen and confidence tricksters and they can operate at all levels, be it as a door-to-door salesman or as a banker who arrives at a meeting wearing an expensive pin-striped suit.

Normally they will offer you some fantastic return on your money and promise you are getting in on the ground floor and could earn 50 times your money by buying this unknown stock which is set to be the next Apple Inc.

Avoid any deals that seem too good to be true.

Sun Tzu said: *If you send men to gather water and they sit and rest and drink before returning then your armed forces are suffering from thirst.*

Put systems in place to track your resources and get alerts when trouble arises.

If you run a business, keep up-to-date accounts and monitor your cash flow situation. If a drop in cash flow indicates a possible problem, address it immediately.

If you're a property developer, monitor your rentals, watching for any difficulties in your ability to rent properties or any spikes in vacancy rates in your area.

Always monitor your personal spending and pay off credit cards in full so outstanding amounts don't lead to high fees and negatively impact your bottom line.

Sun Tzu said: *If the enemy has found an advantage but does not make a move to secure it then you may conclude that his forces are weak and suffering from exhaustion.*

When you see an opportunity and do not seize it right away, consider the possibility that you're suffering from exhaustion.

If you feel constantly stressed and suffer from the feeling of being disillusioned or helplessness then you may be suffering from exhaustion.

You might find that you are in a situation where you feel mentally and physically drained to a point where you can't seem to get yourself out of a tailspin or rut.

Take steps to regain your balance by first looking at your priorities and making time to rest and recuperate. If you are too tired to do this yourself then seek support from those around you.

When you are stressed the effect can spill over into every part of your life, including your health. Your body can become more vulnerable to health issues and you are more likely to get sick, especially if you are unable to sleep well.

When you know you are suffering from stress address the issues causing such stress as quickly as possible so they don't lead to long-term effects that are much more difficult to resolve.

Some causes of stress are related to feeling that you have little or no control over your work or your work environment, or feeling that your efforts are not appreciated.

If you are not inspired or challenged by the work at hand you may be discouraged by its monotony and dread facing it each day.

You may also feel stressed if you feel you can't relax or take time to socialize because you've become a workaholic. You are trying too hard to please too many people and thus feel like you have a mountain of responsibilities. You might also lack social support and feel you have no one you can talk to about your troubles.

A quick check list below might help you see where you are:

- Are you feeling tired and drained on a daily basis?
- Do you suffer from frequent back pain, or muscle aches or spasms?
- Do you feel you've lost your appetite and find it

difficult to sleep well?

- Do you suffer from minor ailments and catch colds easily?

- Do you feel a sense of failure or have feelings of self-doubt?

- Do you feel defeated, trapped, or have a sense of helplessness?

- Do you suffer from a sense of feeling detached and alone in the world?

- Do you lack motivation?

- Do you have a negative outlook on life and feel very cynical about the world?

- Do you find that you have a decreased sense of satisfaction and your accomplishments are empty?

- Do you find yourself avoiding responsibilities?

- Do you find yourself avoiding other people and often stay home or keep to yourself?

- Do you find yourself procrastinating and making excuses and putting things off?

- Do you find yourself eating junk food, taking drugs, or drinking alcohol to numb yourself?

- Do you find yourself lashing out at other people and later feeling guilty about it?

- Do you find yourself coming in late to work and leaving early?

If you can tick off more than 50 percent of these then you may be suffering from exhaustion and/or depression.

Remedies that you may want to consider:

Take ten minutes each morning to drink something warm, slowly, and appreciate any pleasant view you can enjoy. Open a window to get some fresh air. Do what you can to connect with nature and slow down your body so you can start the day energized. If you do this every day you will find that your spirits will begin to lift.

Get in to a healthy routine. Eat foods that provide the energy you need throughout the day. If you have very little time to exercise or go to a gym then take the stairs in your office building rather than the elevator and try to go for a quick walk around the block during lunch time.

Prioritize your task list so you do what's most important first and other matters are scheduled for later. Ask people with new requests for your time and attention to come back later if you are already busy. They will be happier with your efforts if you're honest about your workload and explain when you can do the work they need. Giving false expectations by promising to do the impossible will only lead to a lack of faith in your ability to cope with the demands you face and lead to more stress for everyone involved.

Find an activity that is not related to your work or business and make time for it. Turn off your cell phone when you do this.

Pace yourself so you're not doing too much.

When it's sunny outside take time to go for a walk.

Sometimes sharing is one of the best ways to get on the road to recovery. Tell a friend about your troubles. You may find this simple step very therapeutic and helpful.

Consider the bigger picture and see if your life has

moved in a direction in which there is now a mismatch between you and your environment. You might want to reassess your goals and priorities.

Ask yourself these questions:

- Do I like what I am doing at the moment?
- Do I need to earn this amount of money?
- Do I need to own this car or this house?
- Do I really want to live in this city?
- Do I still feel passionate about my chosen area of expertise?

These are some basic questions that can help you reassess your goals and priorities and lead you to take steps toward positive change in your life

Sun Tzu said: *A general who takes his opponent lightly and does little thinking before attacking will surely be captured.*

Avoid making assumptions about anyone or any situation. Work from facts alone.

Focus on asking the right questions that help you solve a problem or understand a situation.

Don't fill in missing information by making assumptions based on preconceived notions.

Ask questions until you've gathered all the relevant facts that allow you to make an informed judgment.

Don't assume a business associate who hasn't responded to your email doesn't want to speak to you. Call him and ask about it. You might find that his computer was down and he couldn't read any of his emails.

Operating on assumptions can lead to wasted time and resources; stress caused by misunderstandings and miscommunication about co-worker or client needs; and lost business opportunities.

You might lose out on a new business opportunity, for example, if you assume a possible client won't be interested in what you're selling. Or you might lose a client if you fail to provide what he needs because you've assumed he'd be happiest with what you consider your best product.

Don't underestimate anyone or any situation. Communicate and gather the facts you need to fully understand what's going on and take the most effective action. Don't make assumptions.

Sun Tzu said: *Soldiers must be treated well but trained through the regular enforcement of orders so following them becomes a habit. This will make your men disciplined.*

Discipline requires routine. Progress can be difficult to achieve if one day you do what you are supposed to do and the next you do something completely different.

If you want to save up for a vacation and on Monday make sandwiches for lunch to save money but then on Tuesday have a big lunch out you are probably not going to achieve your goal very quickly.

To make a habit stick you need to make it part of your daily routine for an extended period of time. Some people say it takes at least two months to form a habit; others say it takes at least three months. What's most important is that the habit is practiced every day so the brain's neural connections can be rewired so one does something automatically.

Small children, for example, learn the saving habit when they're given a piggy bank or money jar in which they can save their quarters. Now it would be a lot easier just to put a $10 bill into the jar in one go but the child would not learn the saving habit that way.

It's better to give a child a quarter and let them put that into the money jar, each and every day. There is something transformative about repetition that helps us develop habits. Children find such a process fun and feel good about the obvious progress they're making when they stick to their saving plan.

It's also true that you get more of what you focus on. So if you focus on saving money you will get more money. Spending 90 days focusing on saving $1 a day will not only allow you to save up $90, it will attune your mind to the benefits of doing so and lead you to think of more ways you can save rather than spend your money.

Michael M. K. Cheung

Be disciplined so you can bring — and keep — successful habits into your life.

X. Terrain

Sun Tzu said: *Insubordination occurs when the men are of strong will but their leader is of weak will.*

Build yourself up so you can handle bigger and better things.

If you're given a $1 billion company to run and you've never managed a business before you will likely fail. However if you've worked your way up through the business ranks and run various companies through the years you're much more likely to be successful when given such a challenge.

Progression is an important key to success. You need to grow yourself as a person. You can see this in action when you play a computer game such as World of Warcraft in which you start a character at level one and have minimal resources like a few gold coins and just a bread knife and you need to kill level-one critters until you reach level two. Once you reach level two your skill attributes go up and you have to fight level-two critters, but you can use more advanced tools such as swords.

In life as in video games, there are no shortcuts. You

need to spend time and effort building your skills and expertise every day so you can grow as a person and do bigger and better things down the line.

Sun Tzu said: *Collapse will occur when the officers are of strong will but the foot soldiers are of weak will.*

The opposite situation may also cause problems.

Carefully consider your resources and modify your plan accordingly so you can carry it out, even if in a reduced form. Simply scale down a project if fewer resources are available.

If needed, a project can be broken down into parts so the most important part can be tackled with currently available resources and another part can be done when additional resources become available.

A successful software developer, for example, might write and release version 1.0 of his software and then later, once he's gotten more funding or staff to help him, he can release version 2.0 with additional features he was unable to include in his original version.

It's better to take such steps rather than rush into a situation unprepared.

Sun Tzu said: *When senior men are upset and angry they will show insubordination and fight the enemy on their own without waiting for their general to issue orders. This will bring about ruin to the army.*

Don't try to take on a project before you are ready; if you lack the necessary skills you will only end up in ruin.

In the World of Warcraft computer game every area has monsters that are of varying skill levels. If you bring your level-18 team to a level-30 area, you are going to get everyone killed.

Sun Tzu said: *If the general is of weak will and lacks authority, if his orders are not clear and he has not given a structure for his senior officers to follow then the ranks will be formed in a messy manner. The result of such a situation is total and utter disorganization.*

Clearly define your goals and plan related tasks accordingly so they can be executed in an organized matter and lead to your success.

Sun Tzu said: *When the general is unable to gauge the enemy's strength, thus allowing a weak force to engage a stronger one, or allows his best men to be placed at the rear, the result is a rout.*

Focus on your strengths and deliver on that narrow band.

Business people apply the principle of the unique selling point (USP).

What is your personal USP?

Are you good at sales?

Are you good at doing presentations?

Sun Tzu The Art of Making Money

Are you good at problem solving?

What is it that you have that other people don't?

Many computer consultants specialize in particular brands of systems which they know extremely well.

Many doctors specialize in a single area of expertise due to the great amount of knowledge required for each.

Many lawyers also specialize, choosing from a long list of legal fields with their own special rules and regulations: criminal, business, corporate, civil, real estate, family, defense, litigation, etc.

Most professionals decide on their areas of expertise based on their own personal USP and the specific skills they have that will likely contribute to their success.

Sun Tzu said: *A wise general who can go forward and attack without looking for fame, retreat without fearing shame, and who's only thought is of the welfare of his countrymen is a true hero.*

Michael M. K. Cheung

You ego can be your undoing, so strive to tackle projects and tasks objectively to avoid the distractions your ego might otherwise create for you.

Many surgeons maintain a distant bedside manner because they need to keep a certain level of detachment from their patients. This detachment helps them operate objectively and not be affected by emotions during surgery.

Sun Tzu said: *If you know yourself and know the enemy, then victory need not be in question; however if you know the nature of the ground you are about to conquer, then ultimate victory will be in your own hands.*

Understand how you operate. Then watch, wait, and only act when conditions are most favorable.

A futures trader, for example, must know his strengths and weaknesses and have mastery over them so he doesn't lose money. He must spend years learning about a particular market and wait until conditions are favorable before he executes his buy orders.

One such trader knows he's only comfortable holding his position for a week and he's only comfortable using five percent of his money per trade.

He limits himself to five percent because he knows he would otherwise over-commit to a single trade.

This trader understands the precious metals market. He waits until the government runs the printing press and then waits to see the gold price react. Only then does he enter his buy orders.

Your success depends on your ability to operate as though you are a well-oiled machine; you need to keep all the parts moving smoothly, including knowledge of yourself, your area of expertise, and your timing.

Michael M. K. Cheung

XI. The Nine Situations

Sun Tzu said: *The art of war identifies nine types of ground:*

(1) dispersive ground

(2) facile ground

(3) contentious ground

(4) open ground

(5) ground of intersecting highways

(6) serious ground

(7) difficult ground

(8) hemmed-in ground

(9) desperate ground

Sun Tzu said: *When a general is engaged in battle on his home ground, that is called dispersive ground.*

Do not put your home base at risk.

Sun Tzu said: *When a general has penetrated into hostile ground but by only a short distance then that is known as facile ground.*

Do your preliminary research before you commit any resources, knowing you can back out easily early on.

Sun Tzu said: *The ground that if secured would provide great advantage to either side is known as contentious ground, which is contested for.*

When there is no clear market leader in a corner of the marketplace, a small player can quickly establish itself.

In the 1990s the mobile telecom business was contentious ground (i.e., to be contended for) and technology giants were beaten to market share by much smaller operations that could do what was needed very quickly and efficiently.

Sun Tzu said: *When the ground has ease of movement for both parties then that is known as open ground.*

This is ground in which all players small and big can work and no one has a clear advantage.

Sun Tzu The Art of Making Money

Sun Tzu said: *When three lands are joined, the person who occupies the land that intersects the other two has the command of the region.*

A local bank lends money to a company called Supplier A and a company called Consumer B.

While supplier A needs Consumer B because it buys its goods, Consumer B needs Supplier A to make and supply those goods.

Both are interdependent but the local bank has power over both.

If the bank were to close its line of credit and lead Supplier A to bankruptcy then Consumer B would be without a supplier.

If the bank were to close its line of credit and lead Consumer B to bankruptcy then Supplier A would be without a customer.

Therefore the local bank has the most control over the

situation and is in the most powerful position.

Sun Tzu said: *When a general has moved his forces into the heart of hostile territory such that he is surrounded in all directions by fortified cities he has entered into serious ground.*

When you have pushed your efforts and invested your resources deep into your area of interest then you are fully committed. Be prepared to compete and win.

Sun Tzu said: *When the terrain gives to chasms, bogs, and marshes, land that is hard to travel then this is known as difficult ground.*

Difficult ground can be likened to an economic environment that's led to high inflation along with wage freezes. People get squeezed on both sides when costs go up while their pay gets cut. A resultant contraction of money supply causes a vicious circle; consumers have less so they spend less which means businesses have less and pay less.

This is the bust part of the economic cycle of economy. All you can do during such times is be very careful with your resources so you can make them last until boom times start to return.

Sun Tzu said: *When the path narrows and you find yourself surrounded by chasms and gorges and your sky is that of solid granite; and if a small number of soldiers were to find you there then they would crush you even if you were a larger force, then that is hemmed-in ground.*

Hemmed-in ground is often encountered when you are in a contracting market in which less and less money is flowing but commitments such as office leases, homes, cars, and equipment remain.

Sun Tzu said: *When you have entered into grounds where the last resort is to fight at all cost then you have entered into desperate ground.*

Desperate ground can be very profitable when one has the upper hand but very costly for others.

An aggressor on desperate ground can take all the time it wants as it circles like a vulture, waiting to pick the weaker opponent off.

While the aggressor is circling, the weaker opponent is getting more and more desperate. Time is an enemy of the weak on desperate ground as they're more likely to make critical mistakes that lead to rich pickings for the aggressor.

Use desperate ground situations for your own benefit when you are able, but avoid entering them whenever possible.

Sun Tzu said: *When you are on contentious ground you should not attack. When you are on facile ground do not stop but keep on moving; and when on dispersive ground do not fight.*

Do not rest on facile ground because there you are exposed.

Avoid wasting your energy by trying to fight your opponent on contentious ground. Instead use all your energy and resources to build yourself up as quickly as possible so you can gain an advantage.

If you fight on dispersive ground you will have less maneuverability, so always direct your battles to somewhere else.

Sun Tzu said: *When you have entered open ground then you should not try to block the enemy's movement. If you find yourself on ground that borders another force then look to create an alliance with them.*

Do not try to block the enemy when on open ground as it does not provide any strategic advantage. Focus on your strengths and your ideal clients. Do not try to be all things to everyone.

Sun Tzu said: If in the heart of serious ground a wise general should look to loot any resources that he can get his hands on as it will be worth ten times that of his own supplies and thus augment his own supplies. When faced with difficult ground a wise general would look to keep apace and march steadily and not encamp.

Tread carefully on serious ground.

March steadily on difficult ground.

Sun Tzu said: *A general who finds himself on hemmed-in ground should look to apply his stratagem, but when on desperate ground time is of the essence and he must fight.*

When hemmed in you need to resort to strategy to escape.

While many retail shops are getting hemmed in by the rapid expansion of the online shopping phenomenon, some are fighting back via new strategies to entice customers. Such strategies include enhancing a store's ambience or offering free services you can't get while shopping online such as manicures and massages.

Sun Tzu said: *When a general finds an advantage he should move forward to capture it; but when an advantage does not exist he should stop and wait until like a hawk he saw an opportunity to strike.*

Take action only if it gains you an advantage.

Sun Tzu said: *When a general finds the enemy to be moving* *against him he should look to see what his opponent holds dear and seize that resource.*

To get what you want, listen and negotiate win-win situations.

Avoid talking too much. Listen.

Sun Tzu said: *Swiftness is the key essence of war and you should look to take advantage of your enemy's inattentiveness and travel by unconventional paths that enable you to launch attacks on his unmanned positions.*

When an opportunity presents itself, act quickly to gain the upper hand.

Sun Tzu said*: A general who is invading his opponent should know that the further he moves into hostile territory the stronger his men's morale will become as they build on their early victories.*

The greater your market share or expertise in an area or field the more virtuous it becomes. Simply put, success begets success. This is the point at which momentum starts to take over from your hard work. Initially a boulder hardly moves despite the great force you exert. But once you push that boulder over the top and to the downward sloping part of the hill then gravity takes over and all your hard work pays off.

Sun Tzu said: *When on the move your army should look to gather food and water and supplies from the surrounding area. They may need to spend time doing this, putting the main campaign on hold while they replenish their resources.*

Keep the pipeline filled all the time by looking for new revenue streams, profitable markets, and other valuable opportunities.

Sun Tzu said: *A good general should always monitor the well-being of his soldiers and should not overwork them. He should always look at ways to boost their energy and strength while keeping them on the move. He should also keep such a maintenance plan impenetrable and unknown.*

Establish a regular maintenance plan to keep all your assets and resources in top condition.

It is more cost effective to keep all your resources and assets well maintained than let them fall into decay and then have to spend a vast amount of time, energy, and money restoring them.

Sun Tzu The Art of Making Money

Sun Tzu said: *If you put your men into situations where there is no retreat then they will surely fight will all their might as death is their only other option. When faced with death your men will surely choose to live.*

When men have been placed in a dire position all their sense of fear is removed and they stand their ground and fight like ten tigers.

By putting something at stake you increase your chances of success due to your own motivation. If you put nothing in then you have nothing to lose and thus are not committed.

Sun Tzu said: *Do not let your men discuss omens and consider superstitious piffle. Then they will fight will the heart of a tiger and fear nothing until death takes them.*

A clear mind is essential to being successful. A clear mind is free of negative energies that cloud understanding and lead to critical mistakes. A clear and healthy mind means that bad luck will be kept to a minimum and opportunities will be maximized.

Sun Tzu said: *When the day arrives and the men find that the orders to begin battle have come, you will find some may shed a tear or two as they say goodbye to their loved ones but once they have looked into their souls and seen their destiny and seen the vision of their general then each man will have no less than the courage of ten tigers.*

Michael M. K. Cheung

Passion greatly increases the chances of victory. Money is just a way of keeping score; there must be a deeper force propelling you to success. If you are able to tap into that passion you will find that your victories will be many and sweet.

Passion can also reveal courage, which might surprise yourself and those around you.

Sun Tzu said: *A skilled military general may use the form of a shuai-juan which is a snake found in the Chang Mountains. When you strike this snake on its head it will fight back using its tail. If you try to strike its tail then you will find it bites with it head. However this snake if you try to take it by the middle it will strike with both ends, biting you with its head and whipping out at you with its tail.*

Is it possible that this form is found in that of men? If two armies were to cross a river in the same boat that was hit by a storm and water was to come onto the boat all the men would take to buckets to move the water as soon as could be possible.

As the human body is formed with unity, the left side helping to balance and work with the right side, so that is what you must consider in the art of war.

If you play only on the offensive then you always will leave yourself exposed by not looking after your defensive positions.

If you play only on the defensive then you always will leave yourself exposed by not looking after your offensive positions.

Master both defensive and offensive play to ensure ultimate victory.

Sun Tzu said: *A general should not just chain the horses to the tree and remove the chariot wheels and bury them. One must do more if they are to inspire the men to battle like ten tigers. Their passion must be found and brought on the field of battle.*

It is not just enough to be intelligent and knowledgeable about your area of expertise; you must have passion, drive, and purpose in order to maximize your chances of victory.

Sun Tzu said: *A general is given what he has, he cannot change that; some of his men are strong and others are weak— he should not try to look to see if he can be dealt a new set of cards or bemoan his lot; he should consider how best to use his men on the battleground that he find himself on. Like water to the vase he too should find his men as fluid and flexible to their terrain.*

Know when to use your strengths and also when to use your weaknesses.

Use your strengths in the most critical of positions and use your weakness when success matters least.

When the economy is strong, for example, you can work on developing your less well-defined skills.

When the economy is weak, you should focus on your core competencies

Sun Tzu said: *A skilled general will manage and lead his army as easily as if he was giving personal instructions and order to a single man.*

Learn to handle the smallest of assets as well as the largest; if you can look after the pence's then the pounds will be well looked after as well.

Understand how to look at things from the ground up so when you delegate you can quickly know if others are doing a good job.

Sun Tzu The Art of Making Money

Sun Tzu said: *A general should always conduct himself with care and secrecy; let himself be the model for his men yet some things he must keep to himself.*

Tell others information on a selective basis.

If you tell your competitor you're having a problem paying a supplier then your competitor may be able to take advantage of that fact.

Sun Tzu said: *A great general must consider the different measures and how they would be applied to the nine types of ground; he should think whether to take the offensive or defensive approach and he should consider human nature and how it will react in such matters. These are a matter of personal inquiry and in the night before dawn should be contemplated.*

The nine varieties of ground must be studied but to be truly a master of them you need to think out of the box rather than consider them as fixed rules.

Learn the business rules of engagement with the nine varieties of ground but be flexible and adaptable so you can apply them fluidly in any given situation. The ability to be flexible and adaptable can be key to your survival.

Michael M. K. Cheung

Sun Tzu said: *When a general has pushed himself and his men deep into hostile lands, the nature of man is that they are brought closer like a brotherhood of men. However if they have only gone but a short way then they may be easily dispersed like pigeons.*

Once you have penetrated deep into hostile territory then you have committed yourself and must follow through to the end.

XII. The Attack by Fire

Sun Tzu said: *When you are looking to attack your enemy you should first check to see if you have the means to complete the task.*

In order to launch an attack you need to have your resources ready.

Keep plenty of cash in reserves and maintain good relationships with friends, business associates, bank managers, and financiers via in-person and online networking.

Sun Tzu said: When you are looking to use fire as a weapon you should check see if the conditions favor such an attack. What season are you in? Is the weather warm and dry; are the leaves and grasses parched with the lack of rain from the pass three moons?

Timing is very important; be aware of the current economic season and wait for the best time to proceed.

Sun Tzu said: *Does the wind blow in the same direction as that of your men; these are the days that you must consider. Then the time to start a fire is here but take care to not begin if you have the winds blowing to you or if there is a feeling in the air that the winds may change.*

It is better to take action in the direction in which the wind is blowing.

When you move along the path of the wind you have the forces of nature working with you; in this way you follow the path of least resistance.

Sun Tzu said: *A wind that comes in the early morning will carry throughout the day but the breeze that come at night can end as quickly as the rain may end on an autumn night.*

Enter into a trend once it has started but not when it's been going for a long time.

All trends come to an end. The trick is to enter into a trend around 25 percent in and leave at about 75 percent in. By doing this you can avoid getting in so early that you have to endure annoying false starts, and you sell out before the trend ends and becomes less profitable.

Sun Tzu said: *When a general wins his battles but does not find rhyme or reason to his orders from his sovereign his spirit and that of his men will wane and unhappiness and stagnation will follow.*

Victory is only a means to an end; without dreams and passion, ultimately victory is empty and meaningless.

Sun Tzu said: *The wise and enlightened sovereign will have a vision and this he must share with his general if he is to inspire his general and his men.*

Sun Tzu The Art of Making Money

Continuously cultivate and build your resource base. Each action you take either adds to your resource base or detracts from it. Do both wisely.

Sun Tzu said: *A wise general will take no action unless he can see a tactical advantage; he will keep his men on standby unless he will gain something; he will only issue orders to attack when placed in a position of desperation.*

Action requires an expenditure of resources, time, and energy. Only engage in action if there is an advantage to be gained; otherwise it will be a waste of your resources.

Sun Tzu said: *A wise general would not put his men to battle for his own glory or be tempted to engage when provoked.*

Avoid engaging in actions just to stroke our own ego. Guard against making decisions just to show off to your friends or business associates. Such actions can be very costly.

Sun Tzu said: A wise ruler knows that anger can change to gladness, like a caterpillar into a butterfly. Unrest can become contentment given time; so a wise ruler should know that an empire once destroyed cannot be rebuilt. The dead cannot rise and be brought back to life. So the wise ruler should always be mindful and keep his empire at peace and his army cohesive but on standby.

Michael M. K. Cheung

Don't act when your emotions are high. A mistake made while acting rashly can't be easily undone.

A poorly chosen or carelessly spoken word cannot be taken back.

A ruined business cannot be restored and a tarnished image is very difficult to restore.

Choose your words carefully and take action thoughtfully. This another way to protect the resources you've built up through the years and remain prepared for challenges yet to come.

XIII. The Use of Spies

Sun Tzu said: *To raise an army of 1,000,000 men and move them across 1,000 miles would surely drain any great nation of its resources. The daily cost of keeping such an army on the move and well fed would surely cost a thousand ounces of silver. There will be commotion at home and abroad and many men will fall by the wayside. Yet foreknowledge enables the wise sovereign and good general to strike and conquer and achieve things beyond the reach of ordinary men.*

Knowing what is happening in the world and the marketplace is critical to making informed choices and taking appropriate actions.

Sun Tzu said: *Foreknowledge cannot be gained by taking to the spirits or by reasoning with one's experience or other method of deduction. It can only be found by talking and gathering from other men.*

Knowledge can only be gained by going out and looking for it.

The closer you are to the source of knowledge, the more reliable it is.

Sun Tzu said: *There are five types of spies:*

(1) local spies

(2) inward spies

(3) converted spies

(4) doomed spies

(5) surviving spies

There are various ways to gain information about the world and marketplace.

By using even one of these types of spies you will gain a significant advantage over those around you.

Sun Tzu said: *Local spies will entail the use of men that inhabit the district of that land.*

Ask people in the know to gain a better understanding of a situation.

Maybe you're considering opening a surfing and rollerblading shop in a small town because you've assumed most people who live near the coast love to rollerblade and surf. After doing some local research, however, you discover your assumption is wrong. All the people who live on the coast in this town are over 65 years old and just love to sit on the beach and drink margaritas. You opt to open a liquor store instead.

Sun Tzu The Art of Making Money

Sun Tzu said: *Inward spies require the use of the officials that work for your enemy.*

Susan told Tom all about the next-generation software she understood her team would soon develop. This information was relayed to Tom's boss, Bill, who invested a lot of time and resources into a similar project. When it turned out that Susan had been deliberately told about a dummy project her boss had developed to try to mislead her competitors while her teams really worked on a revolutionary tablet PC, Tom and Bill realized they'd lost any momentum they might have had in that area.

Sun Tzu said: *Converted spies are those that spy for your enemy but have been turned to work for you.*

Friends who work for your competitors can often provide you with valuable information if you make it worth their while.

Sun Tzu said: *Doomed spies will do certain things out in the open which will be used as a vehicle for deception. This information can then be gathered and relayed back to the enemy.*

Pamela told Henry over lunch about the new car technology her team was working on. She said they were using the A7 Chip which Henry had thought was still in development. Henry went back to work and told his boss about the other team's use of the A7 Chip. His boss reacted by wasting weeks of his team's time looking into the possibility that they could also use this A7 Chip technology. Meanwhile Pam's team, which had no plans to use the technology, got far ahead of Henry's team.

Sun Tzu said: *Surviving spies bring back news from the enemy's camp.*

Amanda worked for DigitalABC Corp and was hired away by C7Chip Corp. Her new employer pays her well due to her experience with the latest technology, which C7Chip Corp has been long interested in developing.

Sun Tzu said: *Keep close relations with your spies and ensure they are well rewarded. In no other enterprise should greater secrecy be kept.*

Reward those you count on handsomely for helping you out but keep such efforts hidden from prying eyes.

In his company's heyday Ursula's boss always made sure she flew first class on business trips and had a company credit card for any trip expenses as well as an extra day off to go shopping when she travelled to a nice location. When the company's budget had to be tightened, he communicated this to her and explained some of these perks would have to be trimmed. Rather than feel slighted and cut back on her efforts, Ursula appreciated his honesty and worked even harder to help her company get through tough times.

Sun Tzu said: *To ensure proper management of them you should be open and sincere and keep good will with them.*

Be straight with those you value most.

Leo's boss, Jenny, always treats Tom with respect and pays him well and gives him time off when he needs it. When Tom lets Jenny down she doesn't reprimand him but reminds him he's a valuable asset and everyone at the company depends on him to help the business stay afloat in difficult economic times.

Sun Tzu said: *Without subtle cleverness, one will not be able to make certain of the truth of their reports.*

Information must be viewed objectively in case it is inaccurate. Validate whatever information comes your way and strive to understand where it was generated and how it was acquired.

Sun Tzu said: *Be discreet and use your spies whenever a situation presents itself.*

Success depends on a constant information flow. Acquiring vital information should always be a goal, but also should the protection of your own information.

Consider Jackson, who was looking to hire employees away from his biggest competitor. To hide his identity, he hired a third-party company to recruit for him on a non-disclosure basis.

Sun Tzu said: *Before looking to destroy your enemy's army or lay siege to his cities, or even if you are looking to assassinate his leader, first gather names of enemy aides, attendants, gatekeepers, and city watchmen through the use of spies.*

Personal assistants, aides, administrative assistants, and others in similar positions of service are always privy to certain information. How you contact them and toward what purpose must remain private as they are the gatekeepers to the leadership.

Sun Tzu said: *Identify your enemy's spies and offer them bribes, provide them with their hearts' desires. By doing so they will become your assets and work as converted spies; they will then be at your service.*

People who are valued assets should always be catered to. Success often comes from creating such a win-win situation.

Sun Tzu said: *It is through vital from a converted spy that you can seek out the services of local and inward spies.*

A person who has worked for a competitor will have more than just skills to offer your organization. He will bring along his relationships as a valuable asset.

Sun Tzu said: *If you need to bring disinformation to your enemy then commission the services of the doomed spy who will gladly carry this to the enemy.*

If one of your business team members has connections at a competitor, snippets of misinformation can be communicated to give your business an advantage. Such a strategy can only be used lightly, however, before the messenger is no longer trusted.

Sun Tzu said: *The converted spy is the most important because he will know the enemy best. It is essential that he be treated with the most tolerance and good will. Without the converted spy you cannot make use of the surviving spy.*

Recruit people to your camp—whether it's your personal social circles, your business team, or your investment club—who are not only experienced but are well connected. The insights and connections they provide you may prove priceless.

Michael M. K. Cheung

Sun Tzu said: *A great leader will use the highest intelligence of the army for purposes of spying and thereby achieve great results. Spies are the most important element; on them depends an army's ability to move.*

Wars are not fought with guns and tanks alone but with the power of information. He who controls the information flow — and thus the most vital information — is able to secure victory. Knowing a single piece of information can make the difference of whether you are poor or whether you will become a millionaire or a billionaire.

Be your own best spy. Stay alert and gather as much information about your competitors, your industry, and your chosen field of expertise to give yourself the greatest advantage.

XIV. Conclusion

Sun Tzu's wisdom has helped me remember I am not at the mercy of market forces and my success is not set in stone. It is a moving target, one that I can control as long as I live the wisdom of Sun Tzu's ideas and practice them each day. Sun Tzu has also taught me the benefits of remaining flexible and always striving to grow and be more so each and every day is richer that the last.

Most importantly I have learned that life is about being proactive and excelling in everything I do whether I'm at work, rest, or play.

I hope you too will be able to live the wisdom of Sun Tzu so you too will live long and prosper and have a full and rewarding life.

Michael M. K. Cheung

Sun Tzu The Art of Making Money

Contact Information

Twitter:

https://twitter.com/suntzumoney

Email:

info@theartofmakingmoney.co.uk

Website:

http://www.theartofmakingmoney.co.uk

www.ingramcontent.com/pod-product-compliance
Lightning Source LLC
Chambersburg PA
CBHW061506180526
45171CB00001B/56